ECHOES

OF

MY FATHER

ECHOES OF MY FATHER

(A Legacy of Empowerment)

by

TOLA ADELIYI

May 2021

ISBN: Hardcover 978-1-9168941-2-9
Soft Cover: 978-1-9168941-0-5
eBook: 978-1-9168941-1-2

To order additional copies of this book, contact:
Tola Adeliyi: www.tolaadeliyi.com or email
order@tolaadeliyi.com
Black Collectives Ltd: www.blackcollectives.deals

TABLE OF CONTENTS

DEDICATION

This book is dedicated to the blessed memory of my late mother, Josephine Oluyemi Adeliyi, a symbol of humility, love and faithfulness. The one whose love for me knew no bounds and whose adoration of and belief in me continue to stupefy me!

And

To my late father, Olatoye Adegboyega Adeliyi: my teacher, devoted friend, mentor, hero and greatest cheerleader. You were the true epitome of success. You were selfless, brave, inspiring, understanding and always giving. Always nudging me to strive for excellence. In life, you towered above all, yet you were humble. In death, you live on continually. You touched every life you came across and left your giant footprints on the sands of time.

Sleep well, beloved father.

And

To God, the source of all inspiration.

HIGH PRAISES FOR ECHOES OF MY FATHER

This book is a beautiful, brilliant read. It is a grand combination of knowledge and life lessons learnt in rich detail. It is utterly fascinating how "everyday" life, self-discovery, and the philosophy of life are captured in the author's simple storytelling. A great book!

Funke Felix-Adejumo

(Speaker, Life coach and Best-Selling Author of over 50 Books)

The essence of being a supreme educator is in understanding that we never stop learning. It's never about the destination but always about the journey. *Echoes of My Father* is packed full of wisdom and humour, but it is the subtitle *A Legacy of Empowerment* that resonates with those of us who are proud to know Tola Adeliyi today. Empowered? Yes, but more: now the embodiment of the sage assurance his father epitomised. A phrase, anecdote, and unassuming observations empower us to reflect on our values, dealings with others, beliefs and aspirations. A must-read for 2021.

David Payne

Former Headteacher, Bromley, UK

"As a parent of teenagers, I am always looking for books to inspire positive change and vision in my children. Having read many motivational books, I have nothing but praises for the author of *Echoes of My Father (A Legacy of Empowerment)*. This book is well written, insightful, and excellently conveys vital life lessons.

I highly recommend this book to encourage anyone, especially teenagers, to reach their full potential. Chapter 2 on 'Leadership' and Chapter 4, called 'Freedom to Excel', are a must-read for all students, teenagers, young adults, and parents genuinely interested in seeing change. Highly recommended!"

Laura Williams

(Parent and Business Owner, Surrey, UK)

"Mr Tola makes a remarkable impact on everyone who treads his path. Not only is he an incredible mentor to me, but my classmates also view him as an important source of wisdom and guidance. He is the epitome of what I think teachers should be. I am blessed to know Mr Tola in real life. Those who do not will get to know him and benefit from the rich knowledge and wisdom he offers through this book. Buy, read, and tell others about it!"

Moza Alzaabi

(6th Form Student, SRS)

"Mr Tola is one of the most genuine and caring teachers I have ever met. He is like a big brother as well. He always had my back whenever I had problems or needed advice. I have often wondered how a person could be so well put together, empowered and influential. This masterpiece provides answers to how he became such an impactful figure in my school community. In it, Mr Tola shares both his father's wisdom and life lessons that significantly contributed to his development, which he passes on to his students. I believe this book will contribute to your development and empowerment as a student, young adult, parent, or anyone who gets to read it."

Mohammed Ahmed Baghoum

(Grade 12 Student, SRS)

"This book is captivating. The author's rich experience, backed by the clever presentation of his father's wisdom, makes the content very practical and relatable. Many of us are merchants of excuses, but Chapter 4 shatters this deception! *Echoes of my Father* should not only be read by young people but by everyone who desires to live a distinguished life."

Tony Michael
(Life Coach, New York, USA)

ACKNOWLEDGEMENT

I wish to acknowledge the invaluable help of the following people who have contributed to the successful completion of this book and my life.

My Sisters, Funlola, Ronke, Ranmi, Sunmola, Fisola, Damisi and Dayo and their spouses. My brothers Damilohun, Fisayo and Tomiwa and their spouses. They are ever supportive of my dreams and aspirations. Thanks a million for your support.

To my friends, David and Elie Payne (brother and sister from another mother). Thank you for your practical demonstration of love and support.

To the late Jim Rohn and Les Brown. True motivators. You both taught me some of life's most vital lessons. Thanks for being the finest mentors anyone could wish for.

To all my students past and present, especially my current year 7SB6, 8SB6, 9SB2, year 9SG3, and year 10 Chemistry boys and girls at SRS, (Niha, Batool, Amarah, Aliyah, Yumna, Maryan, Arta, Raheema, Hessa, Saffiyah, Shamma R, Maitha, Buthaina, Shamma H, and Bader, Mohammed Bin F, Ahmed N, Abdulla F, Junaid, Asrar, Hassan, and Ayaz). Are there happier and more progressive students anywhere in the world? What would I have done without you guys? You all promised me you would work harder, and you are doing just that. Your confidence in me inspires me.

To Toyin Onabowu of *Heritage Editors* for your painstaking work of editing this book and your constructive advice.

To Oluwabonilarajuasolo (Boni), Oluwakanyinsolami (Kanyinsola), Karis (The "BKK Squad") and my goddaughter, Iris Wiggins. Precious jewels. Thanks for all your contributions and for believing in me!

And to Ewa, ever there! You are by far God's greatest gift to me. Thank you for everything, including the first round of proofreading!

Above all, the sacrifice and praise of my heart and lips go to God, the plenipotentiary, for it is His grace that made it all come true.

FOREWORD

This is the second book of Tola's that I have had the privilege to read and upon which to comment. *Medicine for the Youthful Mind* and this fantastic volume share common features in discussing aspiration, hope and action. Most of all, they speak of love: the love of life, family and all with whom we cross paths.

In this insightful and delightful reflection and testament to the father who helped shape so much of Tola's life, one thing is clear. Alongside his high aspirations and strong belief in their future was the late Mr Adeliyi's unconditional love for his children. This is also true of my friend. He is empathic, thoughtful, and entirely giving himself and time, never more so than when working to maximise young people's life chances.

I could say since I have known and been inspired by this wonderful colleague and friend, I never had the privilege to meet his father, but having read this book and knowing Tola as I do, that would be a falsehood. Every time our paths cross, Tola may not be wearing his father's oversized shoes, but he walks, talks and loves in the light his father left behind.

Tola says this book, like his last, is written to inspire. Inspire you; it will.

Mark A Bennison, FRSA

(International Schools Senior Inspector, Dubai)

INTRODUCTION

It was a sunny Saturday, June 11, 2011. I had gone to work on a piano project with one of my friends, Newton. We were putting together piano chords to support some popular songs to aid children's learning. Everything was going on smoothly until my phone rang.

It was my immediate younger sister, 'Damisi.

"Bros…" She started to say, then she went quiet for a while, then started crying.

I knew something terrible had happened.

In between her tears, "Our father just passed away!" She finally managed to mutter before going silent again. All she did was cry until she hung up.

"Oh my God! Daddy, Daddy! Daddy!" I yelled. I could not find any other words.

As I sat with my hands on my head, tears rolling down my face, Newton eventually understood what had happened and tried to console me.

"I have to leave," I said. Picking my car keys, I drove home. A massive void engulfed me for the rest of the day. My hero had passed away.

On Monday, I headed to school, planning to be strong and get on with life. But I struggled. I broke down and cried in the middle of my year 9 science lesson at The Hazeley Academy, a secondary school in Milton Keynes.

My students' reactions reminded me why I chose this profession.

"Sir, can we give you a hug?" one of them asked. They had never seen me so shaken. Before I could say yes or no, the whole class surrounded me in an embrace of love and empathy.

Shortly afterwards, Mark Bennison, the school principal, walked into my classroom. With a warm handshake, he commiserated with me.

"Go home." He said.

I will never forget that kind gesture.

Since I had promised my year 8 science group a fun practical to consolidate the knowledge from a previous lesson, I refused. After my last class for the day, I went to Mark's office.

"Thank you for dropping in earlier," I said with a heavy heart. "I need a week off to travel for the funeral."

"How old was your father?" Mark asked, gesturing for me to take a seat.

I told him.

"How would you describe his legacy?"

I looked up. "If I could be half the father he was to my own children, I will judge myself a successful father. He left a legacy of educational excellence, integrity and forthrightness. He was the most caring, loving and giving person I ever met."

"Knowing you and what you represent to the students, I am not surprised," Mark said. "He must have been a great man."

Yes, my father was indeed a good and great man. He was my most significant childhood influence.

"Let us not deceive ourselves. His shoes are too big for us," Fisayo, my immediate younger brother told me tearfully during the funeral, which was attended by over 4000 people. "We can only try our best to continue his legacy of excellence, integrity and love."

He was right. Dad's shoes were so big, his influence extended far beyond his immediate family.

After graduating from university, I had started a company with one of my friends. In searching for deals, we submitted a contract bid that I signed on behalf of my four-month-old company. As I left the client's office and got into my car, the director's personal assistant called and told me that the director wanted to see me.

When I entered his office, the man asked where I was from. "Do you know a Mr Adeliyi? Some refer to him as 'The Principal'."

"He is my father," I replied.

He broke into a wide smile. "Is that so? Then I don't need any other assurances." Right there, he swept aside the other quotations, some of which were from well-established and reputable companies. "You have the contract."

I didn't know whether to shout, jump, or start dancing. "Thank you very much for your kind consideration." I managed to blurt out.

He offered me a cold bottle of Malt beverage and the contract. "Your father didn't know me when he helped me." He said. "Without his support and mentorship, I probably would not have got to this position."

"The levels we attain in life will be proportional to the value we put in others."
Olatoye Adeliyi

That was how I obtained my first business contract. How magical a name was, and how true it is that the good or evil men do lives after them.

I told my father what happened when I got home. But he didn't remember the man or the instance, not because he had a bad memory, but because he sowed into people's lives without keeping records or expecting any favours back. That evening marked a turning point in my life. I realised the good seeds we sow may affect the next generation and resolved that my life must be impactful.

My father was never short of precepts, wise sayings, witty expressions, and unforgettable quotes, his own and some from books he had read. He introduced me to some authors including Jim Rhon. He also led by example. This book magnifies and develops his ideas, advice, guidance, quotes, and warnings to me as a child, teenager, and young adult. Some are lessons he taught my siblings and me during our formative years, which became the bedrock of who we all turned out to be.

His death hit me hard because he was not just my father; he was my friend, coach, mentor, and greatest cheerleader. He made his children believe no mountain was too high to surmount and no river too vast for us to cross. His belief in us almost gave us "superpowers". His wise words and advice continue to echo within my heart and mind, giving me direction and inspiration to break barriers.

My life was greatly enriched through exposure to my father's love and encouragement, as well as through reading. Some books were not worth the time spent on them, but others gave meaning to my existence and made me more focused as I journeyed through life. I should be grateful if the words in this book help my students, teenagers, young adults, parents, and anyone else who might read it. I am convinced you are holding a powerful force, and I trust you will be as serious about reading this book as I have been about writing it.

Most books are written to entertain or inform. My desire is that *Echoes of My Father* becomes a tool to fashion a path with worthy goals to help you attain whatever good thing your heart desires. This book is written to inspire and empower you. I hope you will find it a sincere presentation of ideas that can bring value to your life.

Enjoy.

CHAPTER 1

SUCCESS -V- SIGNIFICANCE

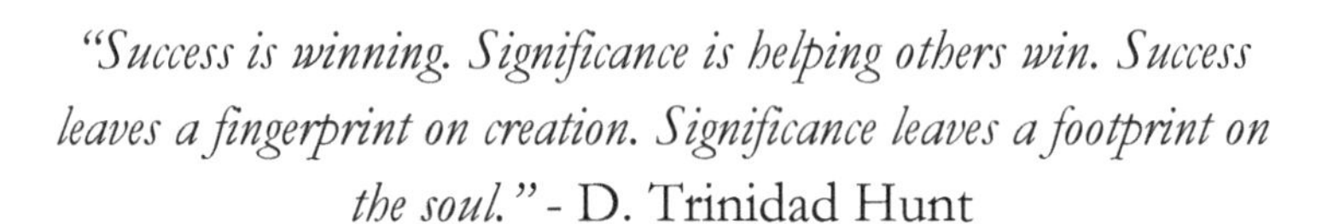

"Success is winning. Significance is helping others win. Success leaves a fingerprint on creation. Significance leaves a footprint on the soul." - D. Trinidad Hunt

When my father died ten years ago, he left behind a legacy of good education, unparalleled love and wisdom that helped the children (biological and non-biological) whom he fathered and mentored over the years. He was a larger-than-life, in our opinion, father in a million; a significant man who sowed and emptied himself into the lives of others. His life and words helped me understand and appreciate life more.

Years ago, I accompanied my father to an ALUMNI meeting with his friend and former school mate, the Chief Executive and Chairman of Cadbury Nig Plc (later the Nigerian High Commissioner to the United Kingdom). Christopher Kolade was a successful and influential man whom I was looking forward to meeting. As we drove into his compound, Kolade himself welcomed us. He stood by the door, smiled, and my father stepped out of the car into his embrace. They exchanged pleasantries while I leaned on the car and watched.

My father signalled for me to come closer. "This is my second son, Olugbotola (my full name from which Tola is derived)." He said. "He is a great admirer of yours."

Kolade smiled and extended his hand to me. We shook hands, and he gave me a hug. "I am honoured, but remember education is the key." He said.

"…and a good life is behind the door!" My father added.

They laughed and walked into the bigger lounge to meet the other guests and start their meeting. While I waited for them in the smaller living room, some jollof rice, served with spicy and tasty chicken, a bottle of soft drink and a 40-inch TV, kept me entertained.

On our way home after the two-hour meeting, I asked my father how it went and who else attended. It turned out that many dignitaries and successful men were there, including the renowned diplomat, Ambassador Ogusulire.

I told my father I couldn't wait to finish university and start journeying into orbits of greatness! In talking to my father about my desire to be successful and what I would do when I achieved my dreams, I was self-centred. It was all about me.

I suspect my father saw through the motives behind those strong desires. Instead of saying "YES! Go for it, my boy!" he firmly and gently said he wanted me not just to be successful but to be significant.

To a teenager driven by the need to make money, get a nice girl, fame and attention, that was a strange concept. I did not fully understand what he meant by significance or what the difference was.

He sensed my confusion. "Tola, you will soon realise that success is subjective.' He said in the unmistakable dulcet tones I was used to. 'Significance, on the other hand, will undeniably change someone's life for the better. Success is about you. Significance is about others."

He wasn't finished. "You often tell me that you easily understand chemistry and love the pattern it presents, right?"

"Yes," I replied, wondering where he was going with this. As I was not in the mood for a chemistry lesson.

"Being able to understand and do well in chemistry is success." He continued. "Sharing your knowledge and helping your friends revise and also do well is significance."

That explanation made things more apparent, but it took many years for the concept to fully crystalise. My motive for success could be about me, but with significance, I cannot be selfish. You see, you can be successful and feel empty. Significance is in the satisfaction that your life is not lived for you alone. I define significance as the transition from selfishness to service – service to others.

> *"There is an emptiness that comes from superficial success." – Olatoye Adeliyi*

Success is reflected in a good university degree, noteworthy title, expensive car, or luxurious house to many people. To some, it is a great business or the ability to mingle with the movers and shakers in society. And to others, it is all about wealth. While those attainments partly define success, you probably know people who tick the boxes but have hollow, unhappy and unfulfilled lives. Fame, fortune, power and the other indicators society celebrates may not amount to success. True success is much more.

My father wanted more for his children. He didn't hesitate to maximise teachable moments, whether in the car on our way to an event or the living room, as he watched a TV program (unless it was the news, which we knew not to interrupt!) Sometimes it was during one of his speeches. He never missed an opportunity to empower, encourage and educate. He understood the power of encouraging rather than negative words.

My father said there is an emptiness that emanates from superficial success. Many who achieve success, as the world defines it, may still feel something is out of place if they have not attained SIGNIFICANCE.

Someone once wrote that "significance allows the internal experience to be as beautiful as the external experience." Significance is in knowing we have had a positive impact on others; that our lives have been meaningful. The conversation, therefore, shifts from one of power to value. How much value can you add to others' lives?

"You can be successful and not be significant." My father continued. "But you cannot be significant without being successful. When you are successful, you have limited influence within a narrow circle. But with significance, your influence can be endless."

I remember telling my father I wanted to become a teacher.

"Good choice." He said.

I could sense his deep satisfaction and pride in me as the phone conversation continued.

"When you influence a child, you influence a life. When you influence a father, you influence a family. When you influence a leader, you influence all who look to him for leadership. Go and start your journey of influence."

If you are dissatisfied with life, check if you add value to others or whether you are merely ruthlessly pursuing success. Everyone is on a journey, and in a few years, we will arrive at a destination. The big question is, where? What destination? The difference between where we arrive and where we wish to be will be in what we are doing right or wrong today. Are your actions contributing to a successful and significant future? Are you of any value to your fellow humans, or are you consumed by the love of self?

We had many intelligent gardeners, house helps, and other low-level workers who did not finish their education because their parents could not afford their basic educational needs. My father never held back from sponsoring them, and many graduated in various fields of endeavours.

No wonder Zig Ziglar, the great motivator, said, "If you help enough people get what they want, you can have whatever you[1]." J. F. Kennedy put it in another way: "Ask not what your country can do for you, ask what you can do for your country."

"Every opportunity to help someone become better is an opportunity to grow, become better and richer." My father said. "Don't wait to make millions before you become useful to others and your community."

My father touched so many lives. He reached out and gave his substance, wisdom and direction to the poor. That was probably why a record 4000 plus people attended his funeral. He was hugely successful because he was significant.

He had a famous saying credited to Jim Rohn: "When the end comes, let it meet you climbing a new mountain, not sliding down an old mountain." At 86 on his sick bed, my father was almost halfway through his sixth book, having written and published five others. He was climbing a new mountain.

Little wonder that on his death bed, at the ripe age of 86, surrounded by some of my siblings, he said, "I have finished my race on earth, I have tried my best, and I am now ready to go with a good conscience. The gates of heaven are opened. Let me go." A few moments later, he passed away.

---

[1] (Ziglar, n.d.)

I miss him every day, for he was my mentor, friend and greatest cheerleader. I am comforted by the path he showed us. I am committed to following and sharing that path to significance and following the more excellent way.

"When you influence a child, you influence a life. When you influence a father, you influence a family." -Olatoye Adeliyi

CHAPTER 2

LEADERSHIP

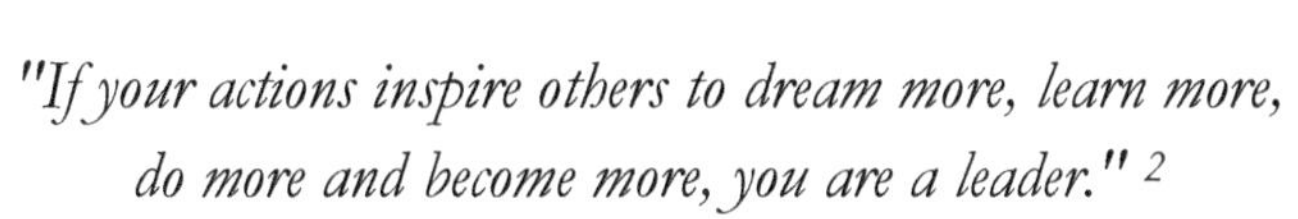

"If your actions inspire others to dream more, learn more, do more and become more, you are a leader." [2]
-John Quincy Adams

I learned a lot about leadership in the last two decades from my father and my mentor, Mr Rohn.

I saw my father welcome both rich and poor into our living room. And I was often with him when he visited dignitaries, including traditional rulers, kings, commissioners, and ministers, in their homes and palaces. He showed the same respect to dignitaries and the less fortunate. Never discriminating, he treated both groups with respect and dignity.

We discussed his leadership style often. I eventually understood why he was so beloved by previous employees, most of whom stayed in touch and attended our functions long after leaving his

[2] (Adams, n.d.)

employment. Many attended his funeral to pay their last respects to a man who gave them so much.

My father told me that a wisely planned life will not simply end with success or significance. It will also be a journey into leadership, and the levels we attain in life will be proportional to the value we put in others. To be significant and add value to another person's life, you do not have to become the director of this or coordinator of that. True success requires you to provide solid directional leadership, hence the need to learn the necessary skills.

Marissa Levin, a culture and leadership expert, agrees with Richard Branson, owner of the Virgin Group, that leadership can inspire and infuse energy, passion, commitment, and connection to an organization's mission[3]. I believe that leadership is the ability to motivate yourself to become worthy of inspiring and leading others. It can sometimes be expressed as the power to influence and persuade someone to adopt a way of life or buy/sell a product. Alternatively, it could be that they have a good idea, and you are working with them to accomplish something worthwhile.

---

[3] (Levin, 2017)

> *"The challenge of leadership is to be strong, but not rude; be kind, but not weak; be bold, but not a bully; be thoughtful, but not lazy; be humble, but not timid; be confident, but not arrogant; have humour, but without folly."*
> *– Jim Rohn*

We all have opportunities and are often already providing leadership and influence. The earlier we understand that and do so correctly, the better for us and those we lead. Those we submit to may not necessarily be named headteacher or president, but they provide leadership. Not all leaders are true leaders, and not all true leaders have a designated position.

As a teacher, you are the leader in your classroom. As a parent, you lead a household. As the first child, you provide leadership to your younger siblings. People look up to you even without realising that they are. They follow what you do, more than simply doing what you tell them.

Jim Rohn made a profound statement that summarises what leadership should be about. He said: "Leaders go from communicating to connecting. Speak, listen, observe, and write. Master those skills. Speaking is not merely talking, listening is not merely hearing, observing is not merely seeing, and writing is not merely scribbling[4]."

If you are a class captain, the head boy or a manager, you must connect with your peers and colleagues. Remember how you got to this place. Do not ignore the people's needs or fail to communicate with them.

---

[4] (Rohn, Uncovering the Two Keys To Leadership Legacy, 2017)

"The tragedy of leadership is in having a short memory". My father told me. "Leaders forget how they got to their current positions, and how they promised to be better leaders when they were under a bad management. They forget how to empathise."

Firstly, identify with the people you are leading - your brother, sister and colleagues. Let them know, not just with talk, but action, that you care for their welfare. It is incredible how many people become leaders and forget everything they promised to do differently beforehand.

If you have an essential idea to share, open a discussion tactfully and thoughtfully. Tact has been defined as the ability to make a point without making an enemy. According to my father, an effective leader must be an astute observer and student of good ideas. Do not let a day pass without seeking answers to questions with the potential to affect you and your team, questions about groups or associations. Who are the new people influencing your world and local opinions? Become competent assessors of events that affect you as they leave a mark on the future.

Extraordinary opportunities are often hidden among life's seemingly insignificant events. They can easily be missed if we do not pay attention and, more importantly, we could fail the people we lead. The more we know these, the more we can nourish and protect them as a mother and father would. That is deep. Protect them like a father. That takes courage that can only be found in true leaders.

In the words of Rob McKenna, "as a leader, you are expected to be many things: courageous enough to take risks and reluctant enough to be real; humble about your accomplishments and convicted about what to do next, and strong enough to lead while open to improving yourself. Sacrificial Leadership in a Self-Centred World requires leaders whose character reflects a combination of selflessness, conviction, courage, integrity, and vulnerability. These leaders know what they want and what is at stake. They work hard at improving themselves and courageously choose to lead despite their healthy reluctance to take the job [5]." And sometimes at personal cost and possibility of losing their lives.

> *"One of the tragedies of leadership is having a short memory. Leaders forget how they got to their current positions, and how they promised to be better leaders when they were under a bad management. They forget how to empathise."*
> *– Olatoye Adeliyi*

An ex-student who attended my father's funeral gave a moving tribute to his courageous leadership. He told the story of how my father once courageously offered himself to protect his students. I was two at the time, too young to remember, so I asked my older sister Ronke Makanjuola, an eyewitness, to throw more light on the incident. She writes:

> "During our father's era as the principal of African Church Teacher Training College, Ifako, a fight erupted after a sporting activity between the students and some military personnel. Consequently, armed soldiers bombarded the principal's quarters where we lived. After attempting to

[5] (McKenna, n.d.)

> spray the buildings with petrol, the military officers barged inside the Principal's quarters, demanding to see him and the offending students and threatening to shoot them.
>
> "Our panicked family members clustered together, praying for divine intervention. We pleaded with Dad not to face the soldiers, but he defied all our appeals and went to meet the military men with his hands raised.
>
> 'Here I am,' he said. 'Shoot me.' He told them he would not allow the unpredictable soldiers to hurt his family or the students in his care.
>
> "With God's intervention and pressures from observers and other stakeholders, sanity prevailed, and the matter was amicably resolved."

A few months after, we were blessed with an addition to the family, a baby girl whom my father named Oludamisi, meaning: "God preserved my life". That showed that he knew the dangers yet chose to put himself in harm's way to protect his students and family. Courageous and sacrificial leadership.

My father constantly reminded me that I needed to be outside the picture frame to see the picture within, implying that you see something in those you lead before they see it in themselves.

Whenever I doubted myself or my ability, my father was quick to say, "*I* see what you do not because you are in the frame."

You must be a parent to those you lead. Bring out the best in them. Steer them from discouragement into positivity. Be ready to give your time and attention. You cannot be selfish and be a good leader.

As earlier stated, John Kennedy, the late United States president, once said, "Don't ask what the country (government, parents, etc.) can do for you, but ask what you can do for your country (parents, school, community)." What can I do for my teacher, mother, father, and son? You do not become successful or develop high self-esteem or recognition by asking what your friend can do for you. Ask what you can do for them.

As a leader, you must get people to work together. You should never be a divisive force. True leaders do not "divide and rule". Getting people to work together is challenging but, once you crack the code, rewarding and exciting. The best approach for a leader, teenager or head of department is not, "you go do it," but "LET'S GO DO IT."

Reward your members. Reward your younger brother or sister, and you may forever change the dynamism of your relationship for the better. The reward may be a handshake, pat on the back, encouragement or a card to appreciate them.

Mark Bennison was one of my headteachers. On my first birthday as a teacher in his school, I found a small card in my pigeonhole that read, *"Dear Tola, you are a rising star at the Hazeley Academy. Thank you for your hard work and dedication to the pupils, and have a happy birthday.* - Mark Bennison"

I was deeply touched and sold on his leadership. After three years in his school, I wanted to move on.

"I don't want you to leave yet." He told me.

I stayed for one more year because of those words, and to date, I still seek his opinion and advice.

Peter Rodin was another great head teacher and leader. In the first three months of being in his school, he came to my office three times to express his appreciation for my work.

"Tola, what I see and hear about you is very encouraging. Thanks for working hard. All the assurances you gave during the interview are indeed true."

The simple but powerful words were the beginning of my deep respect and admiration for him. They made me determined to work even harder. If either of these men asked me for help at 3:00am on a non-school day, I would attend to their requests. That is leadership that encourages and acts with integrity. As opposed to those who look you directly in the eye, lie to your face, and still sleep well at night!

> *"Character is not how you act when people you respect or want to see you in a good light are around. It is how you behave when no one is around."*
> *– Olatoye Adeliyi*

My father did not always say more than a "thank you" whenever we did anything commendable. However, during a public speech, he would highlight a desirable trait or commend us. It was always magical. That's the power of encouragement.

If Jane or I can do it, so can you

Inspire by your testimonies, and help them see themselves as better than they are. Johann Wolfgang von Goethe, the German poet and playwright, once said, "If we treat people as they are, we make them worse. If we treat people as they could be, we help them become what they are capable of becoming[6]".

My father never treated us according to our immaturity, shortcomings, or lack of understanding. Instead, he magnified our capabilities and potential. He was the greatest cheerleader one could ever wish for.

Help those you lead to see themselves clearly, correcting them if mistakes occur. Explain how they missed the mark, but do not leave them in a mess. My father never overlooked our mistakes; in fact, he was a disciplinarian. He raised us with a perfect blend of love and discipline. He skilfully separated the person from the error and helped us become better. What that produced in us was a desire to do the right thing. We obeyed him, not out of fear, but love and the desire to please him. Separate the person from the sin. Let them know that you love them but hate their actions.

Life responds to people who deserve it, not just people who need its help. Do the same by helping people who deserve your help and attention. Also, do the following to lead effectively:

Become A Good Listener: Good leaders are patient listeners. A leader who does not listen carefully will struggle to be influential and inspirational. I cannot remember my father ever dismissing our contributions outright. He listened carefully before giving

[6] (Goethe, n.d.)

thoughtful responses. Listening can be difficult in today's world because various voices continually want our attention.

Jim Rohn once wrote, "It is, therefore, our responsibility to try and be careful with the things we listen to." Whenever we hear these voices, which may be from those we lead, we must stop and assess the messages, not ignore them without considering them. If, after consideration, the suggestion is without substance or not moving towards your goal, tactfully move on. When the message is valuable, process it and see how it might benefit you and your group.

Good listeners become better communicators. Some leaders do not even have the patience to wait for you to finish your sentence. Such people will give the impression that they know it all or are too busy to have time for you. Listening is an opportunity to add to knowledge and increase in value.

"If we fail to set aside the time, if we fail to pick up the book, if we fail to exercise the discipline, then ignorance will quickly move in to fill the space." J Rohn

Be well informed: A leader must be sound in knowledge, so read as many good books as possible. Men and women have offered their experiences in written and spoken form to inspire, instruct and amend our thinking patterns with their ideas. Their contributions enable us to re-plan our lives and avoid their errors. Learn as you go along, knowing others will also look up to you.

Isaac Newton, the great English physicist and inventor who is regarded as one of the most influential scientists in history, said, "If I have seen further (than others), it is by standing upon the shoulders of giants (who came before me)". Newton used understanding gained from prominent thinkers to progress and offer the leadership he became known for.

Reading is essential for those who seek to rise above the ordinary. Do not allow anything to stand between you and that potentially life-changing book. A little reading each day will quickly result in a wealth of valuable information.

Lastly, study leadership patterns. There is nothing wrong with learning from great leaders. There are many leadership styles and strategies to choose from. How you lead is your decision, but you MUST lead.

Atilla the Hun led by fear and intrigue. He was hated by his men and eventually stabbed in the back by his wife. Mobutu Seseseko terrorized his men. Many model leaders inspired love in their followers because they led by example and with love. Sheikh Mohammed bin Rashid Al Maktoum, the ruler of Dubai, once said, "There is a world of difference between a leadership that is based on love and respect, and one that is based on fear[7]." Unfortunately, many leaders in the world have no desire to lead with love or in the interest of their people.

A great leader leads by example and serves the people. Service first to those who deserve it, and then to those who need it.

My father recommended five main qualities (the first five below) that must be found in leaders. I have added a few more gathered

[7] Mohammed bin Rashid Al Maktoum (n.d)

over the years. Consider whether you have these qualities and see where you need to make amends.

1. Vision: Can you see the big picture for you and your team?
2. Purpose: Do you have enough reasons to keep going when people say "no?"
3. Rapport: Are you respectful and responsive to your team members and colleagues?
4. Action: Will you do what you must do?
5. Service: Do you help those who deserve your help?
6. Belief: How certain are you of the validity of your mission or the project at hand?
7. Excellence: Will you settle for less than the best or constantly demand improvement? Will you quit before you get to your destination?
8. Teamwork: Do you recognise the synergy of people working together?
9. Communication: Are you mastering the skills of listening and communicating?
10. Commitment: Are you committed to your team and organisation?
11. Confidence: Are you confident you will make it?
12. Health: Do you take care of your body, soul, and spirit?
13. Love: Will you remember that in the end, love is all that really matters?
14. Sincerity: Will you lead through integrity, or will you follow in the way of the multitude?

These questions beg for answers. A true leader must be a servant leader with these qualities and more.

Lastly, it would be remiss of me not to share the necessity of the leader not to send feelers of defeat to their teammates. I learnt that lesson from a dear friend in France a few years ago when I was leading a team of over 2000 in a multinational marketing company based in Little Rock, Conway, Arkansas, USA.

According to my father, it has been said that "if you are up, go down, and if you are down, go up". One beautiful thing is that leaders also have leaders we respect in our chosen field who should (theoretically at least) know more than we do. It is to them that we turn when we feel concern, anxiety or depression.

Do not adversely impact the people you lead by sending negativity down the line. Avoid sharing angry complaints and depression with your team. When you are "up" emotionally is the best time to talk with those you lead. Do not, and I repeat, DO NOT share your depression and tears with juniors in your team. A considerable percentage of your organisation could be poisoned. It can also be discouraging when a colleague discovers that his leader is uncertain or emotionally down about a course of action. A depressed team leader will make him doubt and question the workability of the project or task.

Ere closing this chapter, I would like to share these sublime words from an email I received on the same issue from Phil Stenberg, a friend of mine from France:

> "Whether in teaching or a traditional business, complaining to your staff is like sawing off the branch you are sitting on. Raising complaints against your subordinates is like setting your own home on fire with

your family locked inside. Your own leaders are for that. Scream, bite, hit, threaten but always to those above you.

"Remember that it is the main quality of a leader to look good as if all is well. Not because you are deceiving them but because you truly believe and know all will be well. Can you imagine the boss of a company, coming half crying to work and saying, 'we are almost bankrupt' or 'we have the worst manufacturing manager!' Would the staff stay? Not even for that day. Then for sure, 100%, that company is dead."

CHAPTER 3

THE POWER OF VISION

"Champions aren't made in the gyms. Champions are made from something they have deep inside them-a desire, a dream, a vision[8]."
—Muhammad Ali

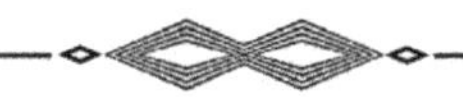

Several factors can shape you as a child. As someone aptly puts it, we are affected by the following 5 C's: Chemistry, Connections, Circumstances, Consciousness, and Choices.

The first C is **Chemistry**. You are affected by your genes. You have no control over your height, eye and skin colour, or other components of your genetic make-up.

The second C is your **Connections**. This includes relationships, particularly during your early impressionable and vulnerable years. Sometimes, it is the kind of parents you have, their careers, schools you attend(ed) or the part of the world you grew up in, and the connections you make during those crucial days.

---

[8] (Ali M. , Champions aren't made in the gyms. Champions are made from something they have deep inside them – a desire, a dream, a vision. ~Muhammad Ali, 2010)

The third C is **Circumstances**. Things that happen to and around you can shape your expectations. The surroundings you live in: some environments support you, others do not. You can also be affected by events – major setbacks, some personal, like the death of a precious family member. You might even be impacted by national occurrences like conflicts and wars or an epidemic like the Coronavirus and the economic woes that come with it. These events, often outside your control, can positively or negatively impact your life.

The fourth C is **Consciousness**. This is how you think about and talk to yourself. It is not just what people are saying to you, but your self-talk. "I am not good enough, too tall, too short, not smart," etc.

The fifth C is **Choice**: This wild card could be a blessing or a curse. Everything in our lives reflects the choices we have made. If you want a different result, choose differently. Simple. It has been said that it is not the cards you are dealt but how you play the hand. That is the choice card. That is in our power. Choosing to do right can make a difference in our lives. None of the other 4 Cs has as much potential to affect the future as making a good choice.

> *"We are our choices."*
> *- Jean-Paul Sartre*

One of my father's common sayings was, "at the end of our lives, the choices we make influence the height we attain." He also often said, "the dreams we allow ourselves to have will determine the course of our lives."

When I opened my business offices, I asked my father to give the opening speech to my invited guests. He never missed an opportunity to impart knowledge. If there was someone who knew my story and how my business began and reached the heights it attained, it was my father. He mentored me through the difficult phases until I achieved success.

In his speech, he said, "whatever we do, the tug of the future must be the most important pull in our lives. Powerful dreams propel you like an iron bar to a strong magnet. The stronger the visions, the more they draw you forward, even through negative events and disasters."

Some people do not recover from disaster because they have nothing left to live for. Nothing on the other side to make life worth living. No dreams to look forward to. Dreams are a projection of the kind of life or impact you want to experience. I am talking about the type of vision that birthed a city like Dubai in the United Arab Emirates.

I came to Dubai for the first time in August 2019 for a two-year contract.

Unfortunately, I had lost my mother in June of that same year. We held her funeral one week before I moved to Dubai. I was missing her, saddened by her loss and burial in the same month of August that my father was buried just 9 years before. However, on leaving the plane, despite my heavy heart and the August heat, I knew I had stepped into a great city. The city of possibilities.

When my daughters asked how the city was, my answer was simple: "Inspiring". I have travelled to many countries on four continents and never been as inspired as I was with Dubai. The reason? It takes excellent vision and the unflinching desire for excellence to transform a desert into a city of distinction. A city determined to be first in fantastic architecture, tourism, and safety. If you have never visited Dubai, come and be inspired.

The type of vision that transformed Dubai is what I am talking about. A concept so clear and so much bigger than the visionary. Cleverly laid out plans and a mind determined to make those dreams come true, even in the face of adversity. A man with a vision has resolved never to give up but rather be transformed by the experiences brought about by adversity. As Sheikh Al Maktoum, the ruler of Dubai, once said, "an easy life does not make men, nor does it build nations. Challenges make men, and it is these men who build nations[9]."

> *"The key is to want something so great and big that it outweighs any trepidation"*
> – *Olatoye Adeliyi*

Someone described dreams as adrenalin injections. "They can make you skip over obstacles or walls that you never thought you could overcome. When you allow your mind to open and your dreams to take wings, they can unleash a creative force that can overpower any obstacle in your path[10]." Note that dreams, not wishful thinking, have the potential to unleash this creative force. Clearly defined dreams. A dream without a future will not have the creative inspiration or pulling power to make things happen. Therefore, to achieve them and have your future aspiration pull you forward, your dreams must be well-defined.

---

[9] Mohammed bin Rashid Al Maktoum (n.d)
[10] Author unknown

The Sheikh of Dubai has already appointed a minister for Artificial Intelligence. That is called planning for the future. Dream big and plan big. We all have nightmares and fears. Let us conquer them with big dreams.

Too Young to dream?

Every time I have a new group of students, I try and get to know them by asking them to share their dreams for the future. Only a few will have a vague idea of what they want to do in the future. Most cannot be bothered.

Then one boy said to me, "Sir, I am only 14."

By the time I was 14, I had wanted to be a principal, teacher, aeronautical engineer, doctor, lawyer, businessman and author. In fact, one of the revision books we used for English in my grade 11 was co-authored by my father, so I wanted to be an author like him. Moreover, watching my father put on his beautiful suits, I wanted to be the principal of a big international school like him. No one could lure me away from those dreams and goals I set for myself. I was too busy trying to grow up and live my dreams. Even though I kept changing what I wanted to become, the dreams made me work harder. At each point, they kept me focused.

Now the big question: Is it too early for a 14-year-old to dream? Or even a 10-year-old? My dreams started long before I was 10. The earlier we start, the better and more focused our lives will be.

Ask your teachers, parents or role models how to achieve that dream. What subjects do you need to concentrate on? What extra classes should you take? Most world achievers started following their dreams very early on in life. Tiger Woods started playing golf at the age of two. The Williams sisters (Serena and Venus, both former world number ones) started playing tennis at 5. Lewis Hamilton began racing remote-controlled cars at 6 and car racing at age 8.

You have to see the future; see the finish line while you are running the race. You must hear the cheers in the middle of an impossible task and be willing to put yourself through the paces of doing the uncomfortable until it becomes comfortable.

Certain voices will remind you of how impossible your dreams are. That best friend, your parents or teacher, could be the unwitting voice. You will hear warnings like "get real". I can imagine what critics and even friends must have told the Wright brothers (inventors of the airplane) as they sought to turn their dreams of flying an object heavier than air into reality. Well did Mohammed Ali say: "Impossible is not a fact, it is an opinion[11]".

It has been said that where there is no vision, the people perish[12]. However, I am amazed today at the number of people who sleep every evening and wake up with no dreams or long- or short-term plan for their lives. Many people plan holidays more meticulously than their lives. When you ask what they want in life, they often reply:

"I want to be successful."

Ask further: "... What would you like to be successful in?" and you become like a barbarian to them. They have no idea what you

---

[11] (Ali M. , Quotable quotes, n.d.)

[12] Proverbs 29:18

are talking about. As far as I am concerned, these people are resigned to fate. They hate their jobs so much that they join the "Thank God it's the weekend!" club. They use the crossed-finger theory of "whatever will be, will be".

If you desire success in any area of your life, begin to dream. And plan towards it. People sit by the computer to plan for their holidays, sometimes two years in advance, but not for their future. Having a dream or vision is as important as the steps towards its realisation. A man without a vision really does not have anything to live for.

It is said that Bill Gates, one of the richest men in the world, was asked for the reason behind his stupendous wealth. He replied that three factors were responsible for his success.

1. Vision and dreams
2. He was in the right place at the right time
3. He took massive action.

Only the first element will be dealt with in this chapter.

Dreams and Visions

All the successful people I know and have studied are men and women of vision. They "saw" long before they saw. Sheikh Rashid bin Saeed Al Maktoum and Sheikh Mohammed Al Maktoum "saw" Dubai in their dreams before seeing its reality. They could clearly see what they wanted before it existed.

When researching for my second book, *Medicine for the Youthful Mind*, I came across the story of Ray Kroc, the man responsible for the global expansion of McDonald's, as told by Wayne Berry. Kroc had a vision of McDonald's as an international franchise operation dominating the fast-food world when he first met the McDonald brothers in Southern California. The brothers believed he was crazy. They had tried franchising and failed, but if Kroc was stupid enough to try where they had failed, they would go along with him; and he could have a percentage of the new company. That percentage was eventually worth billions of dollars to Ray Kroc, who, unlike the McDonald brothers, was not at all surprised when McDonald's succeeded on an astounding scale.

Bill Gates saw that the future of computers was in the software, not hardware. In the 1950s, Walt Disney saw a Disneyland where people worldwide would come to play. This in a world where amusement parks were messy places staffed by shabby people. The bankers Walt approached simply could not see it. The project was said to be laughingly referred to as "Disney's folly", but Walt did it anyway.

I am sure we are all aware of at least one of the Disney Parks around the world. No one is laughing at Walt or his ideas anymore.

> *"Impossible is not a fact, it is an opinion."*
> *- Mohammed Ali*

So, what is your vision? What do you want to achieve in life? The starting point is to see it in your mind's eye. Your mental attitude must be brought in line with your vision. There must be a complete reorientation. If you desire a particular lifestyle, you must do things differently to get the results you want; results that will be directly related to the habits you have formed. Your habits result from consistent actions, which stem from the right mental attitude about what you consider right and essential.

It has been said that if you plant a thought, you should harvest an action. If you plant an action, you will reap a habit. Plant a habit, and you will harvest your character. Plant a character and harvest a destiny. Many have sealed their futures with negative thoughts that became actions, habits, and character that eventually sealed their destinies. How sad for those who do not realise we are the product of our thoughts and deeds.

Let your thinking pattern be more positive. The good news is, the race of life has not ended. You can still live and achieve your dreams. The right mental attitude towards life will guide you to make quality decisions, plan, and adopt the right philosophy in your everyday life, business, and relationships.

We all want success in every area of life, to grow personally and professionally on our journey to success, and live honestly while doing so. Your imagination is always the first step towards the miracle of possibility. That elusive grade A*, B, new job or business is achievable.

Reality starts with imagination. Imagine the possibilities; then imagine that some of them are possible for you. What produces faith? Dreams reassure our faith. Sometimes, stories demonstrate that your dream is achievable. I never cease to tell my students how former students destined for failure turned their lot around. I do so because I know it generates faith and makes them believe that "if James can do it, so can I." So, keep reading and keep listening.

Look in the mirror and tell yourself it is possible. Write down your goals and aspirations, tell yourself you can do it, you can make it, and you *will* make it. Furthermore, turn your faith confessions into action. Affirmation without action is the beginning of self-delusion. I believe we are all presented with many good ideas, some of which may be ours or shared with us by friends, with the potential to create bright futures for us. The problem is that, unlike Bill Gates, who took action instead of just talking about his dreams, most people, even when they recognise that they have a good idea, do nothing.

Mario Cuomo once said, "there are two rules for being successful. One, figure out exactly what you want to do, and two, DO IT[13]".

> *"Success never comes to look for you while you wait around. You have got to get up and work at your dreams to make them come true"*
> *—Poh Yu Khing.*

.I once told a student I was impressed because, unlike many, he had a dream and vision for his future. I advised him to go one step further by laying out plans to achieve that dream and start doing SOMETHING about it.

Talk is cheap. Work hard at your dreams.

---

[13] (Cuomo, n.d.)

CHAPTER 4

THE FREEDOM TO EXCEL

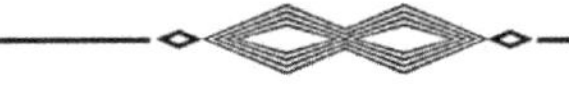

"The wall that keeps out sadness and disappointment is the wall that keeps out joy and fulfilment. It is the same wall."
- Olatoye Adeliyi

A while ago, I visited the Ann Frank house and one of the war camps in Amsterdam, where over 200 thousand people died during the Second World War. People were imprisoned, killed, and sent to death camps because of their beliefs and heritage. Their dreams were cut short, and they were trapped behind those prison walls. Their worlds crashed for something they had no control over.

What a terrible place to be.

Even as I reflect on the evils that created a system so unjust and deadly, I think of our free society today. But how free are we? Are we exercising the freedom to expand our minds and explore the worlds around us? Are we free to be who we want to be, or have we built walls around ourselves and dreams?

Those captured and unjustly imprisoned during present and past wars and uprisings could not live up to their potential even if they wanted to. They could only dream of freedom. It is noteworthy that some did not allow the walls or isolation to stop their dreams.

Like Anne Frank.

Ann Frank was a German-Dutch diarist of Jewish descent. She gained fame posthumously with the publication of her diary, *Anne Frank's Diary*. She and her family went into hiding for a few years to avoid being captured, but that did not cut short her dream of becoming a writer. Anne continued to write, and her writings were published after her death. The walls could not hold her dreams down.

You and I are free from shackles, but are you free in your mind to pursue your dreams and unleash greatness in you? My father once told me people do not live up to their potential because they build imaginary walls around themselves.

> *"Do not always wait for people to inspire you before you do the right thing. They may not show up."*
> *- Olatoye Adeliyi*

What imaginary barriers are stopping you from pursuing your dreams? Are you being held back by past experiences, failures, self-criticism, or feelings of worthlessness and negativity? Or by walls of external criticism from classmates or work mates? Some critics point out only what you do wrong, never what you have done right. They never support you where you have faltered.

My father once quoted, off by heart, the following powerful words by Theodore Roosevelt, former United States president:

The Man in the Arena

> "It is not the critic who counts, not the man who points out how the strong man stumbles or where the doer of deeds could have done them better. **The credit belongs to the man who is actually in the arena,** whose face is marred by dust and sweat and blood; who strives valiantly; who errs, who comes short again and again, because there is no effort without error and shortcoming; but who does actually strive to do the deeds; who knows great enthusiasms, the great devotions; who spends himself in a worthy cause; who at the best knows in the end the triumph of high achievement, and who at the worst, if he fails, at least fails while daring greatly, so that his place shall never be with those cold and timid souls who neither know victory nor defeat."

Powerful. I had it printed and stuck to my wall during my university days until I could recite every word.

The walls

Is your wall that of rationalising things? If the Wright brothers had rationalised their project, there would never have been aeroplanes.

Perhaps doubt is the mighty wall stopping you. People have told me they have good reason to erect a wall and be doubtful: past experiences have taught them to be careful. Maybe that is true, but remember, that same wall keeps out both sadness and disappointment and joy and fulfilment. It is the same wall.

It is time to break down or leap over the walls. As long as they exist in your mind, you will never become the person you are meant to be. You must be hungry for success, such that your desire to break the walls down is more important than anything else. However, never forget that significance is the ultimate goal.

The key is to want something more significant than your fears and invincible walls. This does not suggest that you will always get it right, but your boldness and desire will take you closer to your dreams. Many people would rather stay in the safety of poverty than risk anything and fail.

It is astounding that millions of people are stuck in jobs they hate, getting paid just enough, so they do not quit and working hard enough to not be fired. They complain about their bosses, the environment and their colleagues, yet nothing is done about it.

They even post these failures on Facebook, thinking that it is the same as doing something about the problem. 80% of your friends may have liked the post but don't really care about it. 19% are glad it happened to you and not them. Do not stay down complaining about what they have done to you. Get on with life before they come back. Never be satisfied with anything but the best.

You will fail your way to success. Remember, If you have never failed, you have never tried anything significant.

"Count all your successes and failures." My father said to me. "What I do not want you to count is the number of times you never tried out of fear."

"Courage is not the absence of fear but rather the judgement that something is more important than fear; the brave may not live forever but the cautious do not live at all." –Meg Cabot

Look at your dreams with fresh eyes and say to that wall or mountain, "You have stopped me moving forward enough. This time, I will move on past you." Big or small, make a start and give your dream a chance.

CHAPTER 5

WORRY, THE DARK ROOM

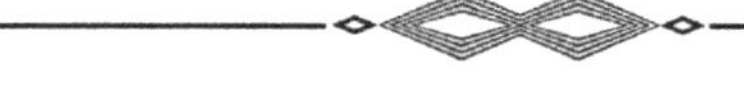

"Worry does not empty tomorrow of its sorrows.
It empties today of its strength.[14]*" — Corrie Ten Boom*

Mothers worry a lot. And good fathers do, too. My father cared enough to be concerned about our safety and outcomes in life. He had a way of projecting calmness, strength, and wisdom in the face of problematic events. My mother was the family's worrier-in-chief. When I left home and travelled the world, my mother worried that something terrible might happen to me. It did not. When I started my first business, she worried that I might not make it. I succeeded after a few years.

When we were young, there was a TV program called *Why Worry?* The main character, named The World Philosopher, had a saying: "Why worry? If you worry, you will eventually die. If you do not worry, you will eventually die. So why worry?"

---

[14] (Boom, n.d.)

My father often repeated his words, "Why worry? Worry time is wasted time." He once told me 99.99% of my mother's worries never came true. That is about the same for mine and, I think, pretty much a universal average.

I loved my mother. She was the most caring, loving, and giving human being I have ever known. In our eyes, she was a saint: St. Worry.

α α α α α α α

I have spent an awful lot of time worrying about grades in school, job interviews, approaching deadlines, etc. I even worried about having my house in perfect condition for visitors. (No one even notices the efforts to make the house extra clean).

Worrying accounts for hours and hours of valuable time I will never get back. And I guess the same might apply to those who worry about upcoming examinations, friends, money, love and even health.

As mentioned earlier, my father always insisted that worry time is wasted time. Why don't you spend the time addressing the situation by studying instead of fretting about your exam? Or talk to your friends instead of wondering what they think about you?

You cannot afford to fret about things that are out of your control. If a situation does not work out as you expect, think of the way forward. And take another shot. Worrying will achieve nothing. Remember, "Life is like a camera, focus on what's important, capture the good times, develop from the negatives.

And if things don't turn out as expected, take another shot!" - Ziad K Abdelnour

Yet, some people agonise over stuff that will never happen and don't move on from the past. Worrying makes you nervous and pessimistic.

Someone once said that "worry is the dark room where negatives are developed". It does not solve anything. Sure, you can be concerned about your financial future and plan towards it; but you cannot worry about things beyond your control.

One more thing: worrying is destructive in many ways. It becomes a mental burden that can even cause us to grow physically sick.

Here are a few strategies for combating worry and maintaining a positive outlook as a student or businessperson.

> *You are the writer of your own life's story. You have the story and the pen, and you can determine the end. It is time to write the next chapter."*
> *– Olatoye Adeliyi*

A. L Williams wrote a book called *All You Can Do Is All You Can Do, But All You Can Do Is Enough*[15], in which he said acting is the secret to success and reducing worry. You must do what you can. Once you have done all you can, it is enough. After that, it is not in your hands anymore. If you honestly do all you can, that is all you can do. Just keep at it. People with worse situations than yours have made it. You can, too.

---

[15] (Williams, 1988)

Hang around positive people – your associations affect your attitude. Turn off the news about the disasters. Go to places (and people) where you can get some inspiration. Worry makes people fearful and irrational. Fear is the expectation that something may go wrong. Fear and worry are cousins. Have faith that things will go right for you.

If fate is what happens to you, DESTINY is what you do with it. Do not worry about fate; take control of your destiny. Do it now. Use your power.

CHAPTER 6
REVENGE

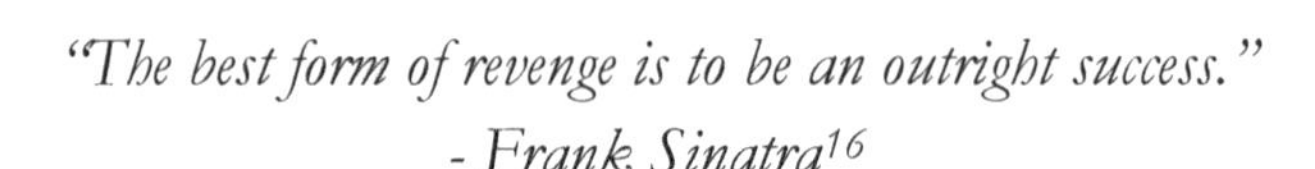

"The best form of revenge is to be an outright success."
- Frank Sinatra[16]

My father taught me about a different type of revenge that I passionately believe in. Yes, at every opportunity, I seek revenge.

What exactly is revenge? I once read a dictionary definition of revenge as a primitive, destructive, and often violent response to anger, injury, or humiliation. It is a misguided attempt to transform shame into pride. It is foolish, unwise and wrong.

So, if it is foolish, unwise, and wrong, why did my father point me in the direction of revenge? I must clearly state that "destructive and often violent" revenge is not the type I believe in; or that my father taught me. I will never subscribe to planning or inflicting hurt for whatever reasons, justified or not. An eye for

[16] (Sinatra, n.d.)

an eye increases blindness, and evil for evil increases evil in the world.

Instead of wasting so much energy plotting to inflict harm or hurt for the wrong you have suffered, devote that energy to improving yourself and becoming a successful puzzle.

Frank Sinatra once said the best form of revenge is to be an outright success. Now that is my type of revenge. Nothing beats it.

We have all been there. We have had people look down on, make fun of, and tell us we do not have the correct height, face, body size, or pedigree to achieve success. The future is not for us; we are a waste of space and do not belong to the destination we seek.

Unfortunately, some people allow those negativities to affect them, dent their self-esteem and affect their outcomes in life. However, a new chapter can be opened when you decide to seek revenge. Instead of building up negative energies, turn them into fuel to power and realise your dreams and achievements.

The new chapter will begin when you are possessed by the desire to prove them wrong for your own good. That desire is backed up by action so that your life can be a beacon of hope to others coming behind you.

So many influential and significant people have shown that if you do not give up or allow people's limited assessments to define you, life will change for you.

Albert Einstein achieved greatness and significance, but his life did not start that way. He did not speak until he was four or read until age seven. His teachers labelled him slow and mentally handicapped and said he would never "amount to much".

Refusing to be defined by how others saw him, Einstein took revenge. Later in life, he won the Nobel prize for his ingenuity in physics. What an achievement! What victory! The boy the teachers said would never amount to much became the face of physics and science in the last century. That is revenge, the way I love it.

Einstein said of his achievements, "It's not that I'm so smart, it's just that I stay with the problems longer ". Do you stay long enough on the task or give up quickly?

Another person who had sweet revenge is **Thomas Edison**. His teachers told him he was "too stupid to learn anything" and gave up on Edison. Edison did not give up on himself. Later in life, this boy became one of the most prolific inventors of all time, inventing the light bulb after one thousand attempts. That is sweet revenge. Thomas Edison teaches that success is round the corner if we do not easily give up. He says: "stories of failure we know of are the stories of those who do not know how close they are to success when they gave up."

Another person who took sweet revenge was **Michael Jordan**. Cut from his high school basketball team for lack of skills, he was so sad, he locked himself up for a few days and refused to see anyone. He did not think of puncturing the PE teacher's car tyres or mounting a resistance against the teacher. Instead, Jordan reinvented himself.

He refused to be defined by the teacher's assessments of him. Years later, after countless hours of practice, development of his skills, and determination, he became a six-time NBA champion, five-time Most Valuable Player in MBA, four-time NBA all-stars champion, and a member of the Olympic gold-winning dream team. Imagine how that PE teacher must have felt as Jordan climbed the ladder of greatness. And how wrong was the coach who thought he knew everything, even Jordan's future? He did not own Jordan's life. It is indeed true that "men can count the number of seeds in an apple, only God can count the number of apples in one seed[17]".

Oprah Winfrey was fired from her TV reporting job because her face was not "fit to be on screen." Her confidence must have taken a hit, but she did not stop pursuing her dreams, later becoming the undisputed queen of television talk shows. Oprah made billions, enough to buy the TV station that rejected her. That is sweet revenge.

Imagine what the publishers who rejected **J.K Rowling's** *Harry Potter* must have felt, having advised her to stop dreaming, get real and get a job. She became more affluent than the queen of England from the sales and endorsements from the same book they rejected many times over. Now that is sweet revenge.

[17] (Schuller, n.d.)

> *"Do not let anyone dictate your potential, the grades you can achieve, businesses you can do, level of success to which you are entitled."*
> *– Olatoye Adeliyi*

Seventeen years ago, when I moved to the UK. I wanted to become a teacher. I loved sharing knowledge and inspiring kids and felt I could make a difference in people's lives and be significant in my own way. I once walked into a university's admission office in England for the GTP (Graduate Teacher Program). The lady in charge took one look at me and told me that they did not have a place. When I asked why she could not give me any reason. She did not ask for my qualifications or experiences; instead, she made her mind up by just looking at me. My face did not fit into her agenda. Of course, she expressed this in the most politically correct way.

I was dejected, feeling that my dream of becoming a teacher in the UK was dying. In the evening, I called my father, who was still alive then. My father patiently listened to me rave and rant and express my disappointment with the system that judged me without giving me the opportunity. He was an excellent listener. My mother could talk non-stop for hours, but my father could listen for ages. That made him so easy to talk to as we knew he would listen carefully and thoughtfully.

After ten minutes, he told me in no uncertain terms:

"Never, ever allow somebody's assessment of your abilities to become your reality. That was her opinion. You are the writer of your own life's story – you have the story and the pen, and you can determine the end. It is time to write the next chapter."

That was the motivation I needed. I started exploring alternatives with renewed vigour.

Over a year later, I qualified as a teacher with a PGCE from a Russell Group University and was offered my first job. Without malice, I drove to her office to say hello, since my job was in the same city.

As soon as she saw me, she repeated the same line. "I told you: we do not have room for you…."

I told her not only was I a qualified teacher, but I had also got my first teaching job. She could not believe her ears. I walked out of her office with my head high. That was my revenge.

People may look down on you. They may call you stupid, ugly, and all sorts of names because you have not made it **yet**. They make you look cheap, and you feel bad about yourself because they appear gift-wrapped, glorious and temporarily better than you are. They call you "a failure" who will never amount to anything.

They knock your confidence so low; you start to doubt your abilities. They do not believe in you and make fun of your dreams. Ah, my friend. Do not let them have the last laugh.

> *"The world is not always going to go your way, it is not designed to do so. If you always respond aggressively to simple occurrences, you may have lost your perspective." – Olatoye Adeliyi*

You have greatness in you. Do not sell yourself short. Shake off the dust, wake the dream up and work hard on yourself and on your skills. Then go after and achieve those goals. All those who made fun of you will marvel at the success story you become!

The best form of revenge is to be an outright success. May you achieve the success you deserve.

CHAPTER 7
TWO TYPES OF PAIN

"I hated every minute of training, but I said, 'Don't quit. Suffer now and live the rest of your life as a champion[18].'"
- Mohammed Ali

As a teacher, I realise that it is difficult to inspire some students. In my fifteen-year career, I have taught in schools in deprived areas that were judged as satisfactory and good and outstanding schools in very affluent areas of the UK. One common factor is some students' inability to connect their current activities to their future outcome and achievements. They do not see the point of most subjects. Some do not even see the point of coming to school, apart from being with their friends. There is no link between what happens in school and their future.

The most unfortunate thing is that teachers and parents try to make these students pay the price when they cannot see the promise. Sacrificing effort and time is hard enough but almost

[18] (Ali M., n.d.)

unbearable when we cannot perceive the need or see immediate results. This is also applicable to adults. We often do not see the "promise" and hence are not willing to pay the price. As a result, success is denied us. Paying the price gets easier and more acceptable if the prize gets more significant or we catch a glimpse of it along the way.

My father was financially balanced, and my siblings and I lived comfortably as children. Once, when we were young, my father drove through poor neighbourhoods. They were not nice areas at all. He told us that the best way to avoid living in such areas was to do well in school, explaining that hard work was why he could afford drive good cars and built houses and live in a five-bedroom house. He also explained that integrity was the reason he could enjoy what he had with peace of mind. I did not fully understand what he did or said, but his actions made me want to take care of **three** things:

1. I wanted to avoid living in the poor neighbourhood
2. I wanted peace of mind.
3. I wanted to drive a nice car when I got older.

In a straightforward but powerful way, it made me focus on my studies. The promise for me was not having to live in a dilapidated house and driving a good car. I had to get it right, and the skills and knowledge to achieve this were attainable at school.

Studying hard to be successful is not easy when you were brought up playing with the Xbox. But what a small price to pay when we consider the promise of a better tomorrow. An ideal situation would be when our parents help us see the promise and encourage us to pay the price. However, we do not always have the ideal circumstances.

> *"If you do not like the results you are getting in life, you are going to have to change. They are your results"*
> *– Olatoye Adeliyi*

Therefore, it is our responsibility as students and adults to understand the purpose of sacrificing so much. Once you do, you will probably be more willing to pay the price. Some time ago, a speaker shared his experience of wanting to give up on his karate lessons. He was fed up and could not cope.

"You cannot believe what it is like to walk up the street alone with no feeling of fear at all." His instructor told him.

The speaker changed his mind immediately. "When do I start the class?"

He had seen the promise and was now ready to pay the price. Some people have the benefit of a father or role model who provides guidance and the necessary motivation. However, many do not have this. The most important thing is to depend less on people to stir you up to do what is right. Self-motivation is priceless. Do not always wait for people to inspire you before you do the right thing. They may not show up.

If you have the proper assurance, you will do whatever it takes to achieve your dreams. If parents or teachers try to make you pay the price before you clearly see the promise, you might resist. What would you do for an extraordinary promise? You would sometimes do the most unbelievable things. You can pay the price if you see where you are going. Would you engage more in your studies? Would you work hard on that project or life-changing exercise?

As life accumulates, we gather the outcomes or regrets of our actions. My father told me that the weight of doing what is right to help you achieve a promising future is light. Regrets about doing the wrong things and ending up on the wrong side of history weigh tons. In the long run, sacrifices are nothing compared to regrets when we do the wrong things. Sacrifices are indeed a small price to pay.

My father always spoke about two types of hurts or pains.

Two types of pain

He said that in life, there are always going to be two types of pains. We must experience one or the other. The first type is the pain of sacrifice. No one can deny that an extra hour or two away from the game machine, friends, or the TV is not a sacrifice for a twelve-, thirteen-, fifteen- or seventeen-year-old. It is a "painful" sacrifice for them. Every successful man or woman I know or have read about went through this. You must also go through this type of pain to make it in life.

Your sacrifice may be the hours spent revising your biology, practising that maths theory or writing that proposal. Sometimes it is taking extra lessons from your teachers. For one past student of mine, the price she paid was going to "Maths help" sessions. She attended these sessions for three years because Math was not her strongest subject. She hardly missed any lessons while all her friends were busy playing or doing other 'interesting' stuff. That was the 'pain' she suffered to avoid the pain of regret. We rejoiced with her as she ended up with a fantastic result and won an award for her effort, focus, and achievement.

I read somewhere that Michael Jackson spent fourteen hours a day practising his dance moves and employed the best to take him through the rigours of that exercise. Little wonder that he was one of the greatest entertainers in the world. For Usain Bolt, the pain of sacrifice was hours of training and perseverance, so he could be the best. Was the sacrifice worth it? Now with millions of pounds' worth of contracts and endorsements, you bet it was.

The other type of pain is **the pain of regret.** These weigh more than the pain of sacrifice. There is nothing as horrible as sitting down and thinking, "I could easily have passed those exams. I could have done better if only I tried harder". It is not a good place to be. Some actions could cost us our lives or guarantee us a room in prison. Yet, they could be avoided. If your friend suggests taking part in a riot, the pain of saying "No" and losing that friend is so much lighter than the regret if you end up injured or in prison.

A student once asked me if it was possible to suffer the two types of pain simultaneously. That is, someone put in the effort and did not make it. My answer was, if you have given your all, then there is nothing more you could do and nothing to regret. If you put in your best, you leave with the satisfaction that you gave it your best shot.

Whatever knowledge or skills you gain will always be an asset for your future. Remember A. L William's book, *All You Can Do Is All You Can Do, And All You Can Do Is Enough?* Doing your best is all anyone can ask.

Unfortunately, humans are about the only organism who put in less than their best in whatever they do. Even a tree will struggle through diseases to grow to its genetic potential. It will grow as tall as possible, and the roots will go deep to find water, often breaking through rocks. But because human beings have the dignity of choice, we often choose to do and, hence achieve, much less than our potential.

This book aims to extract you from this group of people who do as little as they can. I cannot emphasise this enough: walk away from them! I will reiterate, this time in Jim Rohn's words:

> "Walk away from the 97%. Don't use their vocabulary, don't use their excuses, and don't use their method of drift and neglect. Let others lead small lives, but not you. Let others argue over small things, but not you. Let others cry over small hurts, but not you. Let others leave their future in someone else's hands, but not you. Walk away. Don't have days like they do, otherwise, you will end up broke and poor. Pennies but no treasures and trinkets but no values."

In 1999, the late Mohammed Ali (formerly Cassius Clay) was voted BBC's Sporting Personality of the Century. What an achievement. To be considered the best sporting personality in one hundred years and win was an achievement of a lifetime. Many years ago, Mohammed Ali made a significant statement: "I hated every minute of training, but I said, 'Do not quit. Suffer now and live the rest of your life as a champion[19].'"

He refused to live using the "BUY NOW and PAY LATER" philosophy, which means enjoying the benefit of goods and

---

[19] (Ali M. , n.d.)

services and paying later with your sweat and (sometimes) blood. That voice that keeps telling you to ignore your revision now, avoid the lesson now, ignore that voice of reason now, and do what feels good to you. But what happens later in life? If you end up in a job you hate, do not blame life. Employers may not always reward hard work, but life usually does.

> *"I hated every minute of training, but I said, 'Do not quit. Suffer now and live the rest of your life as a champion.'"*
> *- Mohammed Ali*

Old and frail before his death, Ali was always referred to as The Champ and respected all over the world. The state of Kentucky built a centre in his honour. Ali did not have to work any longer. The endorsements provided him with an income for life. He suffered back then but lived as a champion until his death.

CHAPTER 8

DO IT ANYWAY

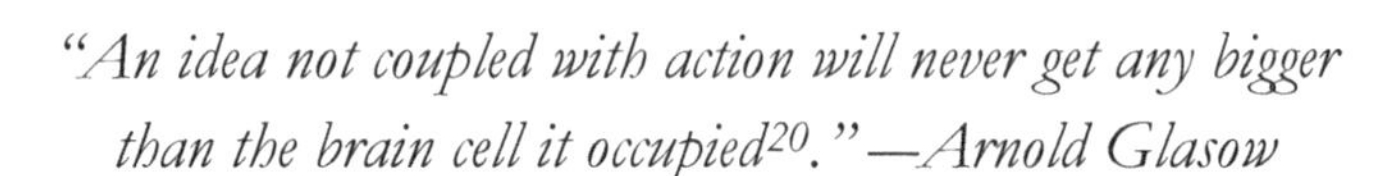

"An idea not coupled with action will never get any bigger than the brain cell it occupied[20]." —Arnold Glasow

When it comes to goals and dreams, FEAR is a major enemy. Think about it. To be fearful when embarking on a new venture is a common occurrence. Everything I have ever attempted and successfully done started with fear.

My father had a simple antidote that he referred to as "*Vitamin do it anyway!*". He never denied the fact that we experience fear. But amid our experience, his advice was to do it anyway.

As stated before, everything I have done successfully started with apprehension and nervousness. I was fearful about my degree examinations, yet I passed; afraid when I started my business, but after a few years' struggles, I succeeded.

---

[20] (Glasow, n.d.)

I was apprehensive the first few times of boarding a plane. Now, with an uncountable number of flights under my belt, fear has never stopped me from going to places I need to go.

I was terrified when I applied to train as a teacher and when I went for my first job interview after qualifying. The same goes for when I stood in front of thirty teenagers for the first time as a teacher.

I was afraid when I went for my driving test and drove on the motorway for the first time. I froze during my first speaking engagement as a motivational speaker. I stood up, but my mind sat down.

I was afraid no one would buy my first book, but it eventually did very well in the market. Then the apprehension returned when I wrote my second book.

Fear. And more fear. Every step of the way, there was fear. I had to overcome trepidation every step of the way. But there is one common denominator. Everything I was fearful of, I went ahead and did anyway.

Why? This is because my dream of getting to my destination without the pains of awaiting a train was greater than the fear of what might happen on the motorway. My desire to impact others positively through words surpassed my dread of speaking in public. That is the only way you turn fear around. And, guess what? It gets easier as you do it. My biggest audience so far was 1,200, and it felt like talking to a few friends because I did it anyway.

The key is to want something so tremendous that it outweighs any trepidation. Then take that step of faith and do it anyway. This does not suggest you will always get it right, but your boldness will bring you closer to your dreams than staying in safety. Many people would rather stay in that safety of poverty and under achievement than risk anything and fail.

If you have never failed, then you have never tried anything significant. You will fail your way to success.

As mentioned earlier, my father said to me, "Count all your successes and count all your failures; but not the number of times you never tried because you were fearful."

It is time for you to look at your dreams again and say to your fears, "You have stopped me moving forward all these years. This time, I will try." Whether your goal is big or small, it is time to start afresh. Your dream may be as simple as moving your grades up, getting a new job, or starting a new business. What you must do now is TRY. TRY. TRY and DO IT ANYWAY!

> "Courage is not the absence of fear but rather the judgement that something is more important than fear; The brave may not live forever, but the cautious do not live at all[21]." – Meg Cabot

Therefore, put your fears aside and DO IT ANYWAY.

---

[21] (Cabot, n.d.)

CHAPTER 9

WHAT IS YOUR "WHY"?

"Inspiration in life is born when we have a purpose"[22]
- Daniel Longwe

Many fathers' desire to see their children do well compels them to control their children's lives by deciding on courses, universities and career paths. In other words, they determine their future. Sometimes it works out well, but at other times, it doesn't, and the children end up stuck in jobs or professions they dislike, working for bosses they hate and getting paid salaries they abhor.

My father never imposed courses or careers on us. He stressed that it was essential to live purposefully and know why we are here in the world. He also outlined the benefits of different opportunities but left us to make our choices and play to our strengths. As with most good mentors, he could see in us what

[22] (Longwe, n.d.)

we could not. As you know, when you are in the frame, you cannot see the picture.

He never believed in the crossed-fingers theory.

"I have my fingers crossed." I would tell him.

"Uncross your fingers." He would reply. "You can keep your fingers crossed for as long as possible, but until you plan and strategize, there will be little progress."

> *He who fails to plan, is planning to fail.*
> *– Olatoye Adeliyi*

Many go through life applying the crossed-fingers theory. Ask them questions, and they will say they are keeping their fingers crossed. I assure you, it doesn't work. What works is a solid plan. But concrete plans are only effective when you understand your purpose.

Mark Twain, the great American author and humourist, put it aptly: "The two most important days in your life are the day you are born, and the day you find out why[23]." What a word.

So, what is your why?

I am convinced that, until you can answer this question, you will go through life careening from wall to wall, living aimlessly and squandering money. You will end up discouraged, concluding that life has handed you an unfair deal.

Knowing your WHY does wonders to your outlook. It will stimulate and inspire you and, what is more, energise you and

---

[23] (Twain, n.d.)

those around you. It makes you build and focus on powerful dreams that can pull you through circumstances and disasters. Some people do not recover from catastrophe because they have nothing to live for and no WHY for living. There is nothing on the other side of the situation to make life worthwhile. Knowing your "whys" makes you settle for nothing less than you deserve. It will make you exit abusive relationships, knowing you deserve better and that your purpose is greater. This knowledge changes the game of life for you.

Your "Whys" make you skip over obstacles or walls you never believed you could overcome. Opening your mind and giving your dreams wings unleashes a creative force that can overpower any obstacle in your path.

I count myself lucky because I found my WHY. The day you discover the reason for your existence will be an exhilarating day.

DO you know your own WHY?

Knowing your why does not bring an end to trials and tribulations. It just means you see things in a different light and have the inner strength to overcome hard times.

Someone wrote these lines, which hit the nail on the head.

> "The day I found out my WHY, life began to take on a whole different turn. It dictated my choices, relationships, value of my time. It determined what I put my effort into

> and the kind of activities I engage in. Life and the world around me instantly became more purposeful[24]."

As you find your WHY, it is equally important to know the WHY for other aspects of your life, e.g. Do you know the WHY for your relationships, job, home (the list goes on)?

This book will meet readers at different points in their lives. Some of you may have just discovered your WHY, and this serves as a confirmation. Or it will inspire you to seek your WHY. Wherever this meets you, I hope you are encouraged to look at things differently, work and walk purposefully. And that you find your sleeping and waking thoughts in an idea or dream.

---

[24] Author unknown.

CHAPTER 10
HOW DO I KNOW MY "WHY"?

"When you find your WHY, you don't hit snooze no more. You find a way to make it happen[25]." -Eric Thomas

I believe everyone is endowed with a gift by the Creator. Everybody has a calling that is tied to a gift. A calling is a strong impulse toward a particular course of action, especially when accompanied by conviction. The Oxford dictionary defines a gift as "a natural ability or talent[26]". It is natural, and you do it effortlessly. Where others struggle, you find it trouble-free. Your gift powers and makes it easy to accomplish your calling.

Your gift/calling is different from your career. Your career is what you are paid for, and your calling is what you are made for.

---

[25] (Thomas, n.d.)
[26] (Oxford Learners' Dictionary, n.d.)

Some people are lucky to be paid for what they are made for. I believe we should all aspire to this.

Let me use myself as an example. Growing up, most of my friends said I had a way with words. I would speak, and friends gathered to listen. I could easily convert any information to humour, motivation and inspiration. I could convert information to deep insight. My desire to impart knowledge was also great. I did not have to try hard – it came naturally.

Therefore, my gift is the ability to use words wisely. My calling is to teach, inspire, coach and motivate people to live fulfilling lives. You will agree that to do that, you need "the gift of the gab," as it is often put. You must have a way with words. This is why I said your calling is tied to a gift.

Now, because I enjoy it, I would talk even if no one was listening and whether I get paid for it or not.

Talking comes naturally and makes me smile, especially when it is for the greater good of humanity. Your "WHY" must make you want to go to work 24/7, inspire passion in you and, better still, if you are paid for it, make you tons of money.

Many people mistake what they enjoy watching or doing as their gifts. For instance, some people have a passion for singing but do not have good voices, even after voice training. Instead of struggling through, their place may be in managing music careers or something else within the music industry that puts them around the things they love.

Jose Mourinho, the former Chelsea Football Club coach, loved football, but he was not a great footballer, so he diverted his deep love and understanding of football into management.

My imperfect guide for discovering your WHY is tied to the following questions that I and many speakers and life coaches use:

1. What makes you smile (People, activities, events, hobbies, projects, etc.…)?
2. What are you naturally good at? (Skills, abilities, gifts etc.)?
3. What activities make you lose track of time?
4. What makes you feel good about yourself?
5. Who inspires you the most? (Anyone you know or do not know. Family, friends, authors, artists, leaders, etc.) Which qualities encourage you in each person? We are often attracted to people with qualities we have that have not been fully expressed in us.
6. What do people typically ask you for help with?
7. If you had to teach something, what would it be?
8. What would you regret not entirely doing, being or having in your life?
9. What are your deepest values?
10. What causes do you strongly believe in? Connect with?
11. If you could get a message across to a large group of people, who would they be? What would your message be?
12. Given your talents, passions and values, how could you use these resources to serve, help and contribute (to people, causes, organizations, the environment, planet etc.)

I believe every WHY must bring deep satisfaction, be easy to do, and geared towards helping humanity in one way or the other. This does not mean that you cannot learn or improve on these skills, but you would spend less time perfecting what others spend two hours on if it is your gift. I sometimes wish school curriculums and systems are aimed at helping students develop their "whys" rather than forcing every subject on them.

> *"Every opportunity to help someone become better is an opportunity to grow, become better and richer."*
> *– Olatoye Adeliyi*

Fortunately, social media and the 21st-century economy have helped millions to monetise their gifts and callings and start living their best lives. And what freedom they experience! What peace and rewards come their way!

Evaluate and make a list of your interests, question yourself, uncover your joy and take action.

CHAPTER 11
TODAY IS YESTERDAY'S TOMORROW

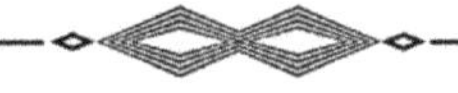

"Procrastination is one of the most common and deadliest of diseases,
and its toll on success and happiness is heavy[27]."- Wayne Gretzky

My father taught me well. I was the chief of leaving everything till tomorrow—no urgency when it came to important things. On the contrary, my extremely disciplined father never left anything that could be done today till tomorrow. He had a sense of urgency to everything, as though tomorrow were not guaranteed. He encouraged us to do the same. One of his favourite sayings was, *"Don't put off till tomorrow what you can do today."*

Perhaps, this is why in all the years I knew him, my father was NEVER late to any event. Not to work, not to social events. The was nothing like "African time" with him. He was always very

[27] (Gretzky, n.d.)

early. He once left my brother and me behind because we were late getting ready. I cried, but the lesson was learnt!

Wikipedia defines procrastination as "the action of delaying or postponing something[28]". The word originates from the Latin *procrastinatus*, which itself evolved from the prefix pro-, meaning "forward," and crastinus, meaning "of tomorrow". Recent studies show that people have more remorse for things they have not done than things they have done. It is therefore undeniable that guilt resulting from missed opportunities stays with people longer.

Napoleon Hill, the great American motivator, once defined procrastination as "the bad habit of putting off until the day after tomorrow what should have been done the day before yesterday[29]". Procrastination has stolen a big chunk from the lives of many potentially great people. How sad.

21st Century students are the most affected by procrastination. Because they have more freedom to make their own decisions, they end up confused about their priorities. Procrastination begins in the morning with pressing the alarm clock snooze button and continues through the day as we get distracted and set crucial things aside. Our dreams soon start to slip through our fingers.

"Shouldn't we have time to relax and work at a later date?" A student asked me after a discussion on procrastination.

---

[28] (Wikipedia, n.d.)
[29] (Hill, n.d.)

"Do not confuse procrastination with relaxation," I replied. "They are two different things. Relaxation recharges your energy, but procrastination drains you. The less energy you have, the more stressed or even depressed you become, and the higher your chances of putting off responsibilities."

I was the master procrastinator. Tomorrow was always the better time to do everything. Not anymore. I acted on my father's advice when he told me the problem with waiting until tomorrow—to do anything—is that when it finally arrives, it is called today.

Seneca, the Roman philosopher, wrote,

> "While we waste our time hesitating and postponing, life is slipping away. Today is yesterday's tomorrow.
>
> The big question is this: What did we do with its opportunities? All too often, we will waste tomorrow as we wasted yesterday… and as we are wasting today. All that could have been accomplished can easily elude us, despite our great intentions, until we inevitably discover that the things that might have been have slipped from our embrace a single, unused day at a time."

I encourage my students and readers to pause frequently and be reminded that the clock is ticking. Exams are drawing near, deadlines are impending. The clock that started to tick from the moment we drew our first breath will cease someday.

Jim Rohn once wrote, "Time is the great equalizer of all mankind. It has taken the best and the worst of us without regard for either[30]."

Time offers opportunity but demands a sense of urgency. When the game of life is finally over, there is no second chance to correct our errors. The clock that ticks the moments of our lives away does not care about winners and losers; or who succeeds or fails. It does not care about excuses, fairness, or equality. The only essential issue is how we played the game.

Regardless of a person's age, an urgency should drive them into action now—this very moment. We should be constantly aware of and value moments that seem so insignificant that their loss often goes unnoticed.

We still have all the time we need. We have lots of chances, opportunities and years to show what we can do. There will be a tomorrow, a next week, next month and year. But unless we develop a sense of urgency, those brief windows of time will be sadly wasted, as were the weeks and months and years before them. There is not an endless supply.

You cannot get rid of time by tearing February out of the calendar, so use the time and opportunity. Charles Richards said, "Don't be fooled by the calendar. There are only as many days in the year as you make use of. One man gets only a week's value out of a year while another man gets a full year's value out of a week[31]."

---

[30] (Rohn, Time Management by Rhon Jim, n.d.)
[31] (Richards, n.d.)

You can waste your ice cream; you can be wasteful and throw clothes away. You can even waste money and make more. But wasted time? That is a whole different situation. I am not talking about the two hours you want back after watching a bad movie. I am talking about the time you feel you wasted watching TV for hours on end, neglecting your English homework, Math revision or that critical deadline.

> *"Dealing with any problem starts with acceptance."*
> – *Olatoye Adeliyi*

And for the older ones, the years wasted staying in a relationship with the wrong person is one of life's biggest regrets, and not because we know we cannot get the time back. We all know that. But because we torture ourselves with what could have been. What you could have done with that time and, as a result, where you would be today. What do we take from all this? A resolve not to waste time and procrastinate any longer.

How then do we break the procrastination cycle? My father always said dealing with any problem starts with acceptance. Therefore, addressing procrastination begins with recognising and accepting that you have that problem. Then find out why you are procrastinating. For example, you may be putting off a task because you find it unpleasant or uninteresting. If that is the case, tackle that task first, so you can focus on the more enjoyable parts of your day.

Poor organisation also leads to procrastination. This can be overcome with a prioritised to-do list. Make sure the list is not too long as to be demoralising. If you have fears about your ability, seek support immediately while completing the tasks you can.

Poor decision-making can lead to procrastination, too. If you have not used the insightful Eisenhower Matrix[32] before, google it and try it.

	Urgent	Not urgent
Important	DO: (Important and Urgent)	SCHEDULE: (Important but not urgent)
Not Important	DELEGATE: (Urgent but not important)	ELIMINATE: (Not urgent and Not important)

As you think of your tomorrow's dreams and goals, take those crucial first steps towards making them come alive today.

It was Mario Cuomo who once said, "there are two rules for being successful. One, figure out exactly what you want to do, and two, DO IT.[33]"

> "Success never comes to look for you while you wait around. You have got to get up and work at your dreams to make them come true."- Poh Yu Khing[34].

Do it N-O-W.

---

[32] https://www.eisenhower.me/eisenhower-matrix/

[33] (Cuomo, n.d.)

[34] (Khing, n.d.)

CHAPTER 12

DO NOT FOLLOW THE MULTITUDES TO DO EVIL (THE POWER OF INFLUENCE)

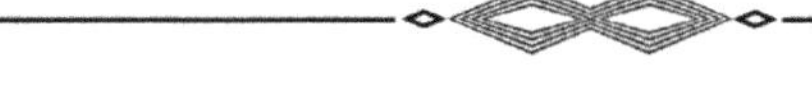

"It is never wrong to do the right thing."- Mark Twain

"Doing the right thing is not always easy. But it is always right." -Tola Adeliyi

I still remember clearly. Our driver took us out to the city centre and parked in the wrong spot with my sister's approval. She allowed him to park there because many other vehicles were parked in the same place. The result was a ticket.

Of course, we had to inform my father.

"Do not follow the multitude to do evil." My father stated in no uncertain terms. "The fact that many people are doing the same things does not make it right. Don't do what feels right, do what is right."

He had a beautiful command of the English language. As a linguist and phonics teacher, his flow of speech was beautiful, even amid his displeasure with our actions. That lesson stuck with me and my sister, Ranmilowo, till today. Every time I am tempted to follow the crowd, the statement echoes in my mind. It has saved me from several bad situations. Mark Twain said, "It is never wrong to do the right thing", to which I add, "doing what is right is NEVER easy, but it is always right." No matter how many people are doing the wrong things, be bold and be the lone voice.

Someone once said that it is easy to stand with the crowd, but it takes courage to stand alone, which we must do if we seek success.

One of my mentors once said and I paraphrase, "Lately, I have been thinking about the power of influence and how the people we are close to and associated with can positively or negatively affect our lives. It is astonishing how many have been destroyed by the associations they keep. My question to our teenagers, youths and even adults is, what effects are your friends having on you?

Ask yourself:

"With whom do I spend most of the time?"

"Who am I being transformed into as a result of this friendship?"

"Are my life chances getting better or worse because of my associations?"

"Are my grades better?"

"What have my close friends got me doing?"

"What have they got me reading?"

"Where have they got me going?"

"What have they got me smoking?"

Make a serious study of how others are influencing you, both negatively and positively.

How many people on your list are achieving their dreams and supporting yours? How many take responsibility for their lives? How many are headed for youth detention centres and prison because of their present attitudes and thoughtless ways?

How many of them are following the multitudes to do evil? Does associating with these people make you or your parents proud? Are you selling yourself short? Or are you on the right track?

You are better off spending time alone than with people who hold themselves and, consequently, you back with a victim mentality. Simply stop spending time with the negative people on your list. You know them. You owe them nothing.

Take responsibility for this area of your life. Look at the people you call friends: you act, talk and have started to think like them. Join the clubs that put you in with a positive circle of friends. Set a new standard for yourself, and do not befriend people who fall below that high standard. Keep successful people around, and you will be successful. Be around people who accomplish their goals, and you will achieve yours.

The Good Book says, "he that is the friend of the wise will be wise, and a companion of fools is headed for destruction[35]". The choice is yours.

I know the desire for acceptance can lead to compromised beliefs and standards, especially for children. Some may feel they are strong enough to resist such pressure, but is this a realistic attitude? Some may find it difficult to accept that, in certain circumstances, peer pressure can be classed as bullying. However, being continuously pressured into acting a certain way for fear of rejection or ridicule might be a form of bullying. Avoid being bullied into doing things you do not want to, and you should not be ashamed to speak out. After all, it is your life's outcome that is at stake.

> *"The choices we make and the dreams we allow ourselves to have determine the courses of our lives."*
> *"Hang around positive people – your associations affect your attitude."*
> – *Olatoye Adeliyi*

To achieve success, you need to start the sorting process. Get all the toxic people out of your life–the energy drainers and dream killers. They do not share your dreams and passion.

My father used to say, "misery is always looking for company". You do not have to provide company for them anymore. State your dreams and aspirations, and allow them to change and be an asset in your life and vice versa.

[35] Proverbs 13:20

All I am advocating here is: take a close and objective look. Everything is worth considering, particularly with the power of influence.

It is easy to dismiss things that influence our lives.

Jim Rhon says, "I live here, but I don't think it matters. I'm around these people, but I don't think it hurts."

"I would take another look at that. Everything counts. Sure, some matter more than others, but everything amounts to something. You've got to keep checking to determine whether your associations are tipping the scales positively or negatively. Ignorance is never the best policy. Finding out is."

While researching for my second book, I came across the story of the little bird who had his wing over his eye. He was crying.

"You are crying." The owl said to him.

"Yes," said the little bird, and he pulled his wing away from his eye.

"Oh, I see," said the owl. "You're crying because the big bird pecked out your eye."

"No, I'm not crying because the big bird pecked out my eye." The little bird replied. "I am crying because I let him."

Many years from now, you may be crying. Not because you ended up poor and useless. But because you allowed it.

CHAPTER 13

THE COURAGE TO CHANGE

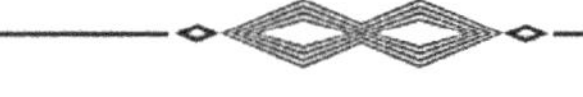

"Change is the only constant thing in life, and the fear of change is also as constant as the change itself." - Heraclitus

Today, when true character is lacking, we must constantly remind ourselves of elements of the human nature that give it more value. One of them, **courage**, is so necessary that it is almost ridiculous not to discuss it.

Nelson Mandela once said he "learned that courage was not the absence of fear, but the triumph over it." He continues:

> "The brave man is not he who does not feel afraid, but he who conquers that fear[36]."

Another variation of that important statement is one I quoted in a previous chapter:

> "Courage is not the absence of fear but rather the judgement that something is more important than fear."

[36] (Mandela, Quotes, n.d.)

> And that "The brave may not live forever, but the cautious do not live at all[37]." – Meg Cabot

What a statement.

Many cannot move forward in business or other areas because they lack courage. Everyone feels fear, but the courageous realise it is not as important as the actions needed to achieve our goals.

The Greek philosopher Aristotle[38] called courage the first virtue because, according to him, it makes all the others possible. In addition, it is the most critical business virtue needed to attain the level of success that we deserve.

Someone once said that innovation withers in the absence of courage. Effective leadership involves making bold and often unpopular decisions. Innovation involves creating ground-breaking, tradition-defying ideas. Sales takes the audacity to be repeatedly rejected before closing a deal. If you take away courage, sales, innovation and leadership lose their potency and appeal. In fact, take away courage, and life seems worthless.

While these types of courage are essential, I conclude with the courage my father emphasised that I needed. He said the most needed courage is to tell yourself the truth about your situation. The courage to be down to earth, look into the mirror and say,

"I have a problem."
"I am not doing as well as I can."
"I am 40 and broke."
"I am 59 and wasting away."

---

[37] (Cabot, n.d.)
[38] (Aristotle, n.d.)

"I am 13 and failing in my schoolwork."
"I live in the land of opportunity, and I am not doing well enough."
"It may not be my fault, but I must do something about it."
"I am 16, and my GCSE is slipping out of my hands."
"My future is gradually eroding."
"I am 15, and I need help!"
"I am going to add knowledge, skills and whatever it takes to make myself more valuable. I am going to become more valuable to the marketplace. I need to change. I will change."

We got there in the end. The courage to change. The courage to do things differently and change the course of our lives.

While changing the way we think and operate is the solution to many problems, humans do not like change. The only people who readily accept change are babies in diapers. Others would rather avoid the word. In fact, according to Nido Qubein, change is an anathema to many. He says, "For the timid, change is frightening, for the comfortable, change is threatening, but for the confident, change is opportunity[39]."

Many see change as the destroyer of what is familiar and comfortable rather than the creator of what is new and exciting. They would rather be comfortable than excellent. But change presents the opportunity to become better and attain better standards of living. How true this is!

Change allows us to become the person that attracts success.

---

[39] (Qubein, n.d.)

What would you do differently today?

My father always told me that "life doesn't get better by CHANCE, or mere confession. It gets better by CHANGE." Not every change will result in improvement, but ALL improvements result from meaningful changes. Meaningful changes result in growth.

My father once shared a story he read about Abraham Lincoln.

It was said that when his mother was about to die, he was by her sick bed. Her dying words: "Be somebody, Abe." changed Lincoln's trajectory. He didn't want to remain the same. He must have taken those words to heart. Little wonder, he did everything possible to achieve his potential. He never gave up despite facing trials and difficulties. He tried and tried and failed many times until he succeeded and eventually became somebody.

You cannot become somebody until you start taking yourself more seriously.

Today, many of us need to be told those exact words because we have settled into being "nobodies". Or, in Zig Ziglar's words, we have become wandering generalities, walking blindly and careening from wall to wall, not knowing what we want in life or how to get there. Wandering generalities instead of being meaningful specifics.

You cannot beat a target you cannot see. If you do not know where you are going, you will probably end up somewhere else. Life must be more than that. You must have goals, plans and crucially, the courage to change your path and work on yourself.

I believe you were created to make an impact, to become somebody in this world. No one should live and die in mediocrity, but it happens all the time. It is time to inspect your life-given gifts, talents, skills, and abilities that may have become dormant over the years. Then do something different to achieve your dreams and goals.

Look at your life: Are you living at your best? Is the person you are right now the best you could be, considering your investments, gifts, talents and ability? Are the results you are producing now the best you could create with the talents and creativity Heaven has given you? If not, it is time to CHANGE. If you do not like the result you are getting in life, you will have to change yourself. Because they are your results. It has nothing to do with your parents, your friends, teachers or mentors. They are your results! Have the courage to CHANGE. Take heed to the words of Abraham Lincoln's mother.

"BE SOMEBODY."

Do you have the courage to embrace positive change today, or would you stay in the safety of poverty and a mediocre life?

CHAPTER 14

KNOWLEDGE IS POWER - WHAT YOU DO NOT KNOW WILL HURT YOU

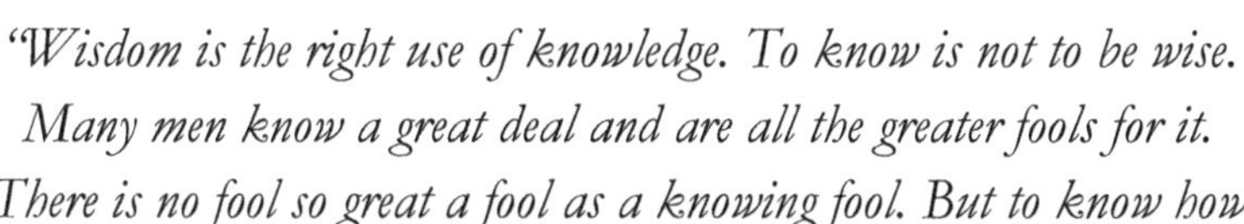

"Wisdom is the right use of knowledge. To know is not to be wise. Many men know a great deal and are all the greater fools for it. There is no fool so great a fool as a knowing fool. But to know how to use knowledge is to have wisdom[40]." — Charles Spurgeon

My father and I spent a lot of time together during the holidays. I volunteered to drive him around in his "chariot". That was the name we gave to his Toyota Crown Deluxe. I did this when his driver was away or on leave. We discussed everything from politics to education. He was always eager to give his opinion and offer his unending wisdom and humour. He had a good sense of humour and was always easy

[40] (Spurgeon, n.d.)

to talk to. Sometimes he brought in profound teachings and admonition from unrelated discussions.

We were driving home from an event when my father suggested passing through the supermarket/pharmacy. Since we had decided to go in, I thought it was a good idea to buy an analgesic rub called *Voltaren* that my mother needed, but they had run out. I told my father that my mother was not aware we planned to buy the rub, so it was no big deal, and it would not hurt her. You know the common saying: "What you don't know cannot hurt you"? Well, my father's response was not typical. It was a teaching moment.

"Wrong." He replied. "What you do not know will hurt you. Knowledge is a defence." He continued. "One basic reason why we learn is to avoid economic, social and personal disasters. We can get hurt by not knowing. Knowledge is power."

We had a long discussion as he shared his insight.

Knowledge *is* power, but only if acted upon. Many men are wise and destitute because they never acted on sound knowledge. Moreover, knowledge and wisdom are different. To know is not to be wise because wisdom is the correct application of knowledge. The deficiency of modern education is the failure to instruct students how to organize and use knowledge after they acquire it.

Ignorance is not bliss

Ignorance is poverty and tragedy. If you don't have information, you can be economically, socially and even physically hurt. One of my mentors once said knowing not to walk out of a ten-storey window is excellent information. If you don't know and walk out on the tenth floor, you will end up dead at the bottom.

So, as I have been taught, I always tell my students: Get all the knowledge while you are in school. Get all the information available. You may not always like it, but learn it. What you do with it is up to you. There is nothing as awful as being out of school and being ignorant.

If you are poor, but you have acquired knowledge, acting on it may well be a way out of poverty and struggles. But poor and stupid? No one can fall lower than that.

Knowledge is power and wealth. Get wisdom, enhance your knowledge, and use both to change your life. Well did Jim Rohn say, "Poor people have big TVs, rich people have big libraries[41]." It is all about knowledge and action!

---

[41] (Rohn, Jim Rohn > Quotes > Quotable Quote, n.d.)

CHAPTER 15

DON'T MAJOR IN MINORS

"Learn to separate the major things from the minor things. People do not do well because they spend major time on minor things[42]."
Jim Rohn

Most of my sisters' children spent time with their grandpa and grandma, at one point or the other. My father had the habit of composing and singing songs to appease and make them laugh. He had adorable pet names for them all. As they grew up, he modified the songs and pet names.

During one of those times, one of my nieces was visiting us at home. I beckoned her over.

"I am busy, Uncle." She replied.

I laughed so hard I could hardly breathe. What important thing was a three-year-old busy doing? She was probably messing up

[42] (Rohn, Time Management by Rhon Jim, n.d.)

the living room and spilling drinks all over the place. However, in her mind, she was very busy.

My father joined me, and we laughed at the adorable girl. Although her being "busy" was part of her developmental process, we agreed that she was busy doing nothing. Her activity was a vital part of her growth, but to us, she was mistaking movement for achievement.

How many mistake movement for achievement? It is easy to be misled into thinking that being busy equals making progress. My father called people like that "Majors in minors" – they are always busy moving around, but they make no progress.

From experience, I realise many fall into the "busy" category. The question is: "Busy doing what?"

One common trait of every successful person is their ability to focus time and energy intelligently. They prioritise what is essential and do not waste time on minor issues. Let me reiterate: if something drains too much of your time and energy, do less of it or avoid it altogether. However, if something feeds and helps secure your future, do a little more of it.

Jim Connolly once said our job is twofold: Discover the key activities that produce the highest returns for us. Secondly, whatever happens, these activities must get done before the lower value tasks. Failing to invest your time correctly means you run the risk of mistaking movement for progress.

Time is of great essence. How we treat this precious gift tells a lot about our lives. It reveals what is important and gives insights into how happy and successful we will become. Time is expensive. When you spend an hour, you are one hour short of the available 24 hours, so use each one wisely. Do not waste, kill or spend it. Invest it.

We can no more afford to spend major time on minor things than spend minor time on major things. Ask yourself the question: *Is this the best use of my time right now?*

If the answer is yes, carry on. If the answer is no, get to work on a more worthy use of your valuable time. So many people waste vital time on what does not add value to their lives: they know who the new neighbours are, who is dating whom, and who owes who or is owed by whom. They are up to date on whose daughter is on what drugs and who is on the detention list in their street.

These people never focus on what could better their lives or edify their fellow men. Take time more seriously and concentrate on what will bring success.

CHAPTER 16

THE PHILOSOPHY OF LIFE

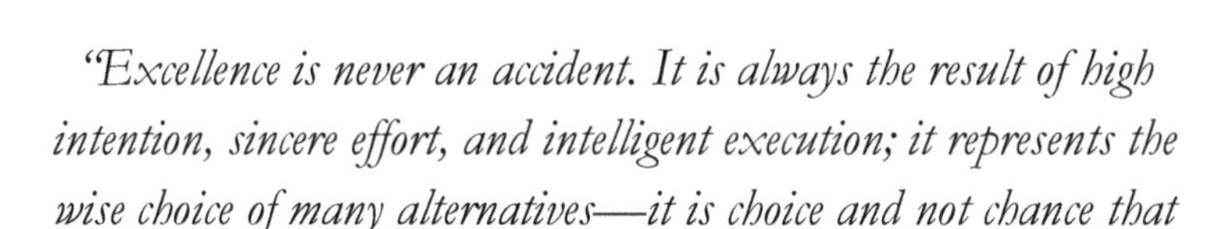

"Excellence is never an accident. It is always the result of high intention, sincere effort, and intelligent execution; it represents the wise choice of many alternatives—it is choice and not chance that determines your destiny." –Aristotle

The quotation above is one of my father's favourites. He believed in and pursued excellence. Nobody accidentally becomes or stumbles on excellence. There must be deliberate efforts to hone our skills. My father was intentional about developing his skills.

As stated previously, he was a linguist extraordinaire. He mastered English, French, German, and Latin. He was awarded the medal of excellence in the French language by the French government earlier in his career. After a dazzling display of distinction in phonetics and the English language, Morehead State University in Kentucky, United States, tried hard to keep him with them after his working visit. He was an extraordinary leader and administrator. His peers referred to him as "the teacher of teachers and mentor of mentors".

More importantly, he was an amazing father. He once told me that, wherever I find myself, I should work hard to be celebrated rather than tolerated. And that if I ever feel tolerated after putting in my very best, it is time to consider my options and take a decision.

He insisted that we must change the way we think and the philosophy we uphold to become successful in whatever we do. Motivation is not productive without the right philosophy. As I grew up and became wiser, I could not help agreeing with him.

You cannot be truly successful and happy without changing your outlook and refining your thought patterns. The information I share here is not just to motivate people to act and do "stuff". It is about motivating someone with the right ideas and philosophy to act in ways that will build a brilliant future.

If you motivate someone with a terrorist mindset, he or she will be out in the street planting bombs and maiming innocent people. You have just developed a motivated terrorist. In the same way, motivate an idiot, and you get a motivated idiot. That is why we need truth to eradicate falsehood and hope to replace despair.

But it is said that sincerity is not the test of truth. You can be sincerely wrong. So, assess truth on the truth scale and sincerity on the sincerity scale. We need a different mindset and a productive philosophy based on the right ideas. To have more and achieve more, we need to know more and become more. This is where personal development and life philosophy comes in.

It starts with the mind. The first change is in our thought patterns. "As a man thinks, so he is[43]." Your mind is the battle ground between voices of negativity saying, on the one hand, "You are too weak, cannot do it, were born poor, no one in your family has ever done it," and the encouraging voice declaring: "Yes, we can! We can achieve the best!"

That is why we must change our thought pattern for a different life. In essence, the most meaningful changes come from within. Unfortunately, as I said earlier, the only person who welcomes change is the baby in a wet diaper. The rest of us are set in our ways, and most would rather remain in the safety of our weak and beggarly existence than change.

It is remarkable how many students accept low grades until the pain of remaining the same exceeds the need for change. In my experience, every single improvement came after changing something within and modifying or getting rid of certain habits.

My father and mentors always told me to work harder on myself than on my job. They also said to work harder than what I earned—if I was paid £10, I should put in £20 worth of work and effort—however, I should work harder on myself than on my job. In so doing, I would build myself up.

I pass the same wisdom to you. Work hard to enhance your knowledge, sharpen your skills, and become a better person. Only then does the marketplace appreciate you. Studying good books and material activates the mind. It is part and parcel of your personal development and change in philosophy. Every

---

[43] Proverbs 23:7

outstanding person I know studies, and every studious person eventually becomes exceptional. You cannot be a committed thinker if you do not study; neither can you think in a vacuum. Fill your mind with good information. Do not spend money on shoes alone, but on building yourself up.

To quote Isaac Newton, again: "If I have seen further than others, it is by standing upon the shoulders of giants who have gone before me." He found inspiration from studying the work of great scientists who came before him. He studied and improved on their material. My father's admonitions and the books I read inspired me. Get inspiration to prepare you for a solid future by reading good books.

As mentioned earlier, what you do not know will leave you ignorant and affect your achievement levels. Books you do not read will not help you. What you do not know ***can*** hurt you and adversely affect your future.

Why do you need to prepare? Because opportunity will show up. When it does, the only thing to do is present your skills, readiness, performance, and talent to opportunity.

One of my mentors said, "You don't present needs to opportunity." It is better to be prepared and not have an opportunity than to have an opportunity and not be ready. Everything you need to develop yourself is available and within your (reading and listening) reach. But who is going to reach out?

Part of personal development is working on character. It is not enough to be knowledgeable and wise. It is not even enough to be a good looking and charismatic student or worker. A solid character must be developed. For character is what is left when charisma is gone. Jim Rohn once said,

> "Character is not something you were born with and can't change, like your fingerprints. In fact, because you were not born with it, it is something that you must take responsibility for creating." He continued, "I don't believe that adversity by itself builds character, and I certainly don't think that success erodes it. Character is built by how you respond to what happens in your life. Whether it is winning or losing every game, getting rich or dealing with hard times. You build character out of certain qualities that you must create and diligently nurture within yourself, just like you would plant and water a seed or gather wood and build a campfire[44]."

Character is not how you act when people you respect or want to see you in a good light are around. It is how you behave when no one is around. What you do, not because it feels good, but because you know it is right. You do it whether you are rewarded or not.

Work on yourself as you work hard on your road to success.

---

[44] (Rohn, Creating Your Character, n.d.)

CHAPTER 17
THE LAWS

"The laws of life set the mind that obeys them free."

The Law of Perspective

Looking back, my father had an interesting way of viewing things. I remember returning home with a heavy heart, usually because of some minor events in school. The questions he asked made me wonder why I was upset in the first place.

One day in grade 7, I came home almost in tears after falling out with my friend. My father asked what happened, and I proceeded to explain at length. He listened actively and patiently to my rants.

Then he asked. "Did any one die?"

"No," I answered.

"Was anyone seriously injured?"

"No!"

"What is the worst thing that could happen? Would you lose your place in the school...?"

By the time he finished his line of questioning, I wondered why I was upset.

I was (I am) alive.

I was (and am) well.

No one died.

My father taught me to be thankful for the important things and let go of insignificant things. Many people get upset about trivialities. They lose their temper over getting stuck in traffic, become distraught because they fall out with friends or someone looked at them funny, or the waiter got their order wrong. Some behave like the world is ending because of a setback in their studies or an exam.

The world is not always going to go your way. It is not designed to do so. But if you always respond aggressively to simple occurrences, you may have lost your perspective.

Travis Bradberry once wrote that "If you struggle with putting things into perspective, just ask yourself two simple questions: What's the worst thing that could happen because of this? Will this matter in five years[45]?"

---

[45] (Bradberry, n.d.)

These are the types of questions my father asked. Today, friends will ask why my reactions to certain situations are often milder than the reactions they are used to.

I always reply, "My father helped me put things into perspective when I was growing up". Even when I am initially angry, the law of perspective kicks in within a few minutes, and the problem seems to become smaller than when I first rated it.

When issues occur, put things in perspective.

The Law of Use

This was one of the first laws my father made me understand. He never failed to magnify what he thought his children's gifts and endowments were, and he encouraged us to utilise them.

"What you don't use, you lose," he said.

My father was our example: He maximised his God-given abilities as much as his energy allowed. He believed and told us that good is the enemy of the best and that good only becomes better through use. He said good becomes better with practice and then becomes best.

Many people stop trying once they achieve a level of success. They become good, forget they can be better, and that being the best is even greater than being better.

That philosophy was what he taught us.

Sometimes, the teaching moments were brought out in ways that made us laugh, but the lessons were hardly missed. One day a friend came to visit me.

My father asked how he was doing.

"I am doing good, Sir," he said.

"You can do better." My father replied.

The three of us laughed. Although my father was joking, he was passing across the subtle message that you don't have to settle for good. You can be better.

Many people do not strive for better once they start doing good. They settle for what they have and stop growing. Use what you have. Don't bury or hide your talent. You will lose it.

If you use your talent, the world will be a better place. As I grew up, I started to understand this law of use in greater depth. I can assure you, as a science teacher that, if you tie up any part of your body and leave it alone long enough, the blood ceases to flow into those places. They stop working, and you will never be able to use them again. Lack of use causes loss.

That is why people who have been active all their lives sometimes develop difficulties of all sorts when they retire. Their faculties diminish when they stop using them as intensely as before.

Interests that are not acted on will diminish. In my experience, if you do not act on a good idea within 24 hours, you are 50% less likely to ever act on it. Within 7 days, you have less than a 2% chance of doing something about that idea. That is true for many human virtues - your brain, desires, dreams, and other human virtues.

If you have a voice, use it. The same goes for unused love, ambition, strong emotions and feelings. Even faith decreases when unexercised. Vitality, energy and courage will all diminish if allowed to lie fallow. Make sure you use your talents. Let me reiterate this point, this time in the words of one of my mentors, Les Brown:

> "Imagine being on your death bed and standing around you is the ghost of the dreams, the ideas, the abilities, the talents given to you by life. That, for whatever reason, you never went after that dream. You never acted on those ideas. You never used the talents. You never used those gifts, and there they are, standing beside your bed, looking at YOU with large, angry eyes saying, 'we came to you and only you could have given us life. And now, we must die with you forever.[46]'"

You have one chance to write your legacy. What will it be? Take charge of your life and make it count.

The Law of Process

Another lesson my father taught me is the law of process. Growth is a process, and no one grows overnight. We need the necessary ingredients, and the process takes time.

"Be careful about overnight success." He often said. "Unless you are born to a wealthy man, overnight success is a misleading concept. People do not succeed or fail overnight. Process gives you the result."

---

[46] (Brown, n.d.)

Failure is what we get from years of making bad choices. As Jim Rohn aptly puts it, "Failure is the inevitable result of an accumulation of poor thinking and poor choices. To put it more simply, failure is nothing more than a few errors in judgment repeated every day[47]."

The question is: why would someone make an error in judgment and then foolishly repeat it every day? Because he or she does not think it matters. On their own, our daily actions do not seem that important. A minor oversight, poor decision, or wasted hour generally doesn't result in immediate and measurable impact.

Those who smoke or drink too much make these poor choices year after year because they don't seem to matter. But the pain and regret of these errors in judgment have only been delayed. If the sky falls on us on the day we make the first one, we would undoubtedly take immediate steps to ensure that the act is never repeated. Like the child who places his hand on a hot burner despite his parents' warnings, an instantaneous experience would accompany the misjudgement. Unfortunately, failure does not shout out warnings as our parents did.

The same goes for success. People don't succeed overnight. The process we follow on our journey to success matures, develops and sharpens our character and personality. It is, therefore, vital to be grateful for the process as well as the result. Process is what a sculptor and the chisel are to the wood. Or what the porter is to the clay. The sculptor chisels out the excesses and ugliness of low self-esteem, pride and arrogance. This is also why some people win the lottery and end up broke a few years later. They

---

[47] (Rohn, The Formula for Success and Failure, n.d.)

won millions but never became millionaires. The process of BECOMING helps the person build character, encounter and overcome failures, and gain valuable experience.

Bill Gates is one of the world's richest men. He has been in the top five for years, but he did not magically build up a vast fortune. He worked for it, experienced failure and learned a lot along the route to becoming a billionaire. Gates' first company, Traf-O-Data, wasn't successful, but it provided a learning experience for Gates and his partner associates. Imagine if Bill Gates gave up a day after he failed? There would be no Microsoft.

CHAPTER 18

DREAM THIEF

"The Dream thief, another name for negative inner conversations, is the reason so many people take their greatness to the grave."

My father often talked about the dream thief. According to him, a thief is lurking around us. In fact, it operates *in* us with one purpose. To stop you from getting to your destination in life.

Whenever you think of an idea that could bring value to your life, the thief appears. As soon as you start thinking of this great thing, the inner conversations begin. These internal conversations are what my father called the dream or mind thief. They are the main reason behind many people's lack of achievement in the classroom, at work, or in life generally.

Some examples of messages from the mind thief are: "I am too old/short/fat/tall/dumb. I have never done that before. I am black or Arab and live in a white country. I am an Asian living in an Arab world. No family member has ever done that before. No one loves me…" The list goes on.

How many people have planned to do something great, positive, and meaningful and then talked themselves out of it? I do not mean your parents or friends. *You* talked yourself out of it. This dream thief always tells you that you are incapable of achieving anything in life. The inner conversation is the reason so many people take their greatness to the grave.

Someone once said the wealthiest place on the planet is not the gold mines in South Africa, the diamond fields, or Hollywood. It is the graveyard. You will find all sorts there. Great ideas that were never developed. Unrealised hopes and dreams. Inventions that were never created and even uncomposed songs. Books never written and published. All because most people let the internal conversation get the better of them, making them ineffectual.

> *"Many people die at age 37 but are not buried until the age of 75. They are dead in their affections and dead without lively dreams and aspirations. They are just not in graves." – Olatoye Adeliyi*

This inner conversation keeps telling you how inadequate you are. No one will ever buy your songs or read your book. You are destined to be ordinary, poor, and oppressed. These conversations are strengthened by past experiences with parents, spouses, or friends who treated you worse than you deserved. In response, you concluded that you are not worth much.

Many people die at 37 but are not buried until the age of 75. They are dead in their affections and lack lively dreams and aspirations. They are just not in graves. Having settled for whatever life offers, their spirits sink further every day.

They do not put in their best in anything because the dream thief has stolen their inner strength. They say things like, "I see, what you mean now, and I will try my best". I know that talk is cheap, but I also know that those who are honourable enough to do what they say can change the course of their lives and the world at large.

If a man does his very best, no one can ask for anything more. If you put in your best, you are satisfied that you gave it your best shot.

Walk away from people who will not go the extra mile or dig in to find the strength to keep going. Expose yourself to positive people and good information, all of whom are within reading and listening reach. Do not be conformed to being an average person but be transformed by the renewing of your mind.

"Don't quit; I will suffer now and live the rest of my life as a winner[48]."

---

[48] (Ali M. , Quotable quotes, n.d.)

CHAPTER 19
BREAKING FROM THE PAST

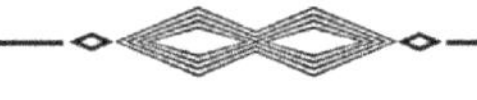

"No matter the strength of their wings,
most never leave their cages[49]." — Jason Versey

The man without a past has no future. We all have a history. Some are prouder of theirs than others. My father was my first example of someone who completely broke free from his past. His foresight and ability to see into the future meant he could not hold on to the past. I believe we will never be satisfied with remaining in our comfort zone once we catch a glimpse of the future.

Although my grandfather was a wealthy cocoa merchant, he was not keen on educating any of his children. My grandmother eventually convinced him otherwise, and my father, who was of school age at the time, went to school and never looked back.

He was not the first person to be educated in his extended family but, as the first university graduate, he opened the door and

[49] (Versey, n.d.)

became a role model for everyone in the family. He even sponsored some of them to achieve the same or similar education levels.

My father was not going to be held back by his heritage or background. People are often held back because of circumstances like where they were born and their family history. Your history does not need to dictate your future. According to Mark Caine, "the first step toward success is taken when you refuse to be a captive of the environment in which you first find yourself[50]."

One of my students in England came to me after doing poorly on a test. She was almost in tears.

"Mr Adeliyi, I will never be a graduate."

"Why not?" I asked.

"There are no graduates in my family. And I am not doing well in my chosen subjects," She replied. "My parents are menial workers."

I told her how my father became the first graduate in his family. "What does your pedigree have to do with your dreams and choices?" I continued. "You can break the cycle if you want to be your family's first graduate."

She looked at me and said nothing.

This girl is brilliant, very academic, but it would be safe to say she had no confidence. She never answered questions during lessons

---

[50] (Caine, n.d.)

but would stay behind to ask questions or come to see me during breaks. Every time I asked her about any concept or topic taught in class, she always replied: "I know my answer is rubbish, but I think..."

Her "rubbish" answers were usually correct and insightful. This was an intelligent student who was much better than she thought. I needed to interrupt the messages in her head and help her realise that her history, which was her stumbling block, did not have to dictate her future reality.

I practised past papers and shared revision strategies with her. She started gaining confidence and, with my continuous reassurance, progressed from the foundation to higher science papers. I shared my findings and approach with her other teachers. She ended up with a B in science, a grade that she never previously achieved or thought possible. When I moved to another school, her family sent me the most enormous chocolate cake I have ever seen.

Stop Press**As I was finishing this book, an ex-colleague who was close to her family confirmed that this student, who was never going to be a graduate, graduated from the University of Liverpool some years ago. I felt blessed to hear the news.*

Your circumstances do not define the person you become. By the end of next year, you and I could still be the same people, depending on the choices we make from now on. I recommend you choose life and say YES to your dream and bright future.

When I wanted to train to be a teacher, a friend advised me to sincerely reconsider my plan. I had what it took and the necessary experience, but how would I teach English children when I came from a different background? Another friend advised me to get a truck driving license because, as he said, "their pay is competitive". Don't get me wrong, there is nothing wrong with being a truck driver if that is your dream, and it would give you satisfaction now and in the future.

> *'Never, ever let somebody else's assessment of your abilities to become your reality – Olatoye Adeliyi*

But that was not my dream.

I love being a part of success stories, and I would do that in teaching. Lack of good progress is not because we aim too high and miss the target. It stems from aiming too low and hitting that target. Then we convince ourselves that we are doing well compared to those who have not lived up to their full potential, and we feel good with ourselves.

Will Smith made a profound statement to his son in his role as Chris Gardener in the movie *The Pursuit of Happyness*: "Don't ever let someone tell you, you can't do something. Not even me. You got a dream; you got to protect it. People can't do something themselves; they want to tell you you can't do it. You want something, go get it. Period[51]."

I followed my dream, and the rest is history now.

---

[51] (Muccino, 2006)

Do not let anyone dictate your potential, the grades you can achieve, the businesses you can do, level of success you are entitled to. People's opinion of you does not have to become your reality. As Muhammad Ali said, "impossible is not a fact, it is an opinion[52]". It is somebody's opinion.

Some people with privileged backgrounds may lose focus along the way. Do you frequently regret previous decisions or actions? Don't beat yourself up too much. We all have pasts. Oscar Wilde puts it this way: "every saint has a past, and every sinner has a future[53]". How true.

Albert Einstein also said, "Anyone who has never made a mistake has never tried anything new[54]." We are all human and prone to mistakes. But you do not have to mortgage your future to one or two past mistakes.

Many of us go through "remembrance stages" where we waste time dwelling on the past and neglect new opportunities that present themselves daily.

> "There may have been many opportunities lost or mistakes made, but those will never return, so you need to let go and go after those opportunities that are constantly presenting themselves to you now. The future is the place you can repair all the damages."

Applaud the fact that you have learned your lesson well. Stop diminishing today's achievements because you have built a shrine

---

[52] (Ali M. , n.d.)
[53] (Wilde, n.d.)
[54] (Einstein, n.d.)

to yesterday's mistake. Leave the past in the past, move on and stop robbing yourself of present happiness. You deserve happiness and health; do not jeopardise either.

I watched a program on YouTube in which the character said he was jailed for making the same mistake only 14 times! Now that is a disease. Your mistakes are only part of the learning curve. Do not miss the lessons they intend to teach you. What you learn can empower others, so do not mess up the opportunity to be a teacher by overlooking the message behind the mistake.

> *"He who does not know his past cannot make the best of his present and future, for it is from the past that we learn." - Sheikh Zayed Al Nahyan*

Past Hurts and Unforgiveness

Holding on to hurts inflicted on you by others may impede breakthroughs in your life. Do not become a slave to unforgiveness. You may think you are justified to be angry and bitter, but you hurt yourself by not forgiving. Nelson Mandela understood the principle perfectly. On being released from prison, he said, "As I walked out the door toward the gate that would lead to my freedom, I knew if I didn't leave my bitterness and hatred behind, I'd still be in prison[55]." That was a profound truth.

> *Resentment is like drinking poison and then hoping it will kill your enemies."*
> *- Nelson Mandela*

---

[55] (Mandela, 9 Inspiring Nelson Mandela Quotes on Forgiveness, n.d.)

Do not deny your past. Defy it. Who you were has nothing to do with who you can be. Many people carry the past as a burden, not as a school. Learn from the past and move on with your life. Your best days are ahead, not behind you. Before ending this chapter, I would like to quote the poetic words from an unknown writer from another age.

> "There are two days in every week about which we should not worry, two days which should be kept free from fear and apprehension. One of these days is YESTERDAY, with its mistakes and cares, its faults and blunders, its aches and pains. Yesterday has passed forever beyond our control. All the money in the world cannot bring back yesterday. We cannot undo a single act we performed or erase a single word we said. Yesterday is gone. The other day we should not worry about is TOMORROW, with its possible adversities, its burdens, its large promise, and its poor performance. Tomorrow is also beyond our immediate control.
>
> "This leaves only one day, TODAY. Anyone can fight the battles of just one day. It is only when you and I add the burdens of those two awful eternities—Yesterday and Tomorrow—that we break down. It is not the experience of Today that drives us mad; it is remorse and bitterness for something which happened yesterday and the dread of what tomorrow may bring. Let us therefore… Live this one full TODAY[56]."

---

[56] Author Unknown

Knowing fully well that "…men can count the number of seeds in an apple. Only God can count the number of apples in one seed[57]", break away and, like a seed, sprout and live a life of abundance.

[57] (Schuller, n.d.)

CHAPTER 20

NEVER GIVE UP

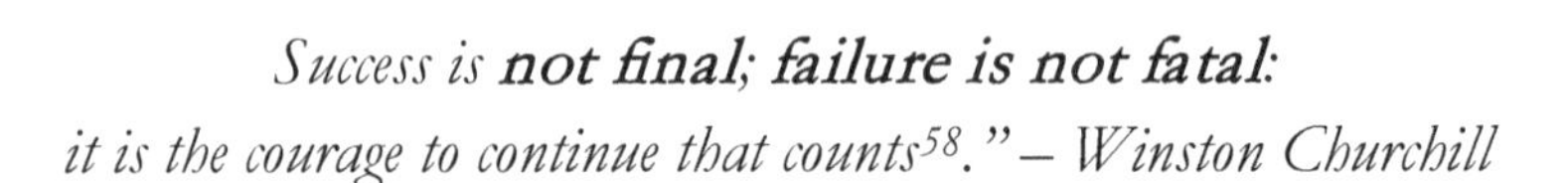

Success is ***not final; failure is not fatal:***
it is the courage to continue that counts[58]*." – Winston Churchill*

Thomas Edison, the great inventor, said, "The stories of failure we know are the stories of those that do not know how close they were to success when they gave up[59]."

I never ceased to be amazed by the number of people who give up on their dreams. I did not understand why people could quit on laudable and achievable goals that could be so rewarding. Then I realised quitting is something we see in every industry. Bankers quit; programmers quit. Teachers quit. In fact, I once read of an IBM interview where 50% of the people who qualified for the interview did not show up. They quit before they started.

---

58 (Churchill, n.d.)
59 (Edison T. A., n.d.)

The temptation to quit does not just apply to you. Most people never make it because they stopped too early. But you can make a difference. Stay committed to your dreams.

> "Failure cannot handle persistence. Persistence always wins in the end[60]."- *Calvin Coolidge*

If there is one significant thing I want you to learn from me, it is not to give up on your dreams. Do not stop dreaming because you failed the first, second or third time. The project failed temporarily, but you are not a failure. The relationship ended, but you are not a failure. Do not stop because someone else does not believe in your dreams or your attempts did not succeed at once.

Edison tried a thousand experiments before he created the first successful light bulb. He eventually became one of the most prolific inventors of all time, with more than 1,000 patents to his name. He later said about his failed attempts at the electric lamp; "I have not failed. I have just found 1,000 ways that didn't work[61]." What an idea. He also said, "many of life's failures are people who did not realize how close they were to success when they gave up[62]." He was a great advocate for hard work. When "asked for his definition of genius [Edison] is said to have answered, "2% is genius and 98% is hard work[63]."

There are countless instances of famous people who made it after years of not giving up. They set good examples, but, generally, man's first instinct under pressure is to run, extricate or remove

---

60 (Coolidge, n.d.)
61 (Edison T. A., n.d.)
62 (Edison T. A., n.d.)
63 (Edison T. , n.d.)

himself from the situation. When we run from a problem or give up, we immediately flunk the test. If we must be winners in life, we cannot be sluggards or quitters. Nothing can defeat us except our own unbelief.

Many years ago, my father gave me an enormous book titled *100 Great Lives*. In this book, with over a thousand pages, I read of a young man who was not given any chances to make it big in life. He had no beauty or charming smile to pave the way for him. In fact, his father's description of him was, "He looked as if he had been badly cut with an axe and needed smoothing with a jackplane."

His goal was to become a member of the legislature. He joined politics, strove manfully, and was defeated. He decided to go into business, but that resulted in bankruptcy and many years spent paying off his crooked partner's bad debt. He started a law practice, and it was a failure. He fell in love with a beautiful woman, and death snatched her away. Then this man decided to be a full-time politician, ran for congress and lost. He ran for the Senate, was defeated twice, became a candidate for the vice-presidency and was rejected.

If anyone had reason to quit, this man did. He had a young son who was the darling of his life. And the boy died. Did he give up? No, even though many a lesser man would have. Today, you can see his determined, sorrowful and compassion-filled face, looking down on the union and slaves he saved from his great white chair at the Lincoln monument in Washington D. C.

Instead of quitting, Lincoln became an over-comer, prevailed and made it to the throne (of the United States of America). Abraham Lincoln, though dead, still speaks to you and me.

Ah. My friend, you may feel you have failed in every opportunity you have been given in life so far. Or that you have messed up every chance of achieving success in your schoolwork and professional life. I have news for you. The race is still on. ***Failure is not fatal:*** *it is the courage to continue that counts.*

We are not made for defeat, and you can still make a difference. Start correcting the errors of the past so that you can make something out of your life. It is better late than never.

Are you at a crossroad in your life? Do you feel overwhelmed with problems at school or at home? Do you feel like a failure? Do you feel like giving up on that dream? You are closer to victory than you imagine.

Strength, my friend, springs out of weakness. Life emerges out of death. Victory is secured in the heat of battle. The 'crown' of success goes only to those who stick with it to the end. Quitters receive no crowns, the fearful go empty-handed, but he who endures till the end shall be successful.

Strength springs out of weakness and life emerges out of death.
–Tola Adeliyi

"If you can't fly, then run. If you can't run, then walk. If you can't walk, then crawl; but whatever you do, you have to keep moving forward[64]." — Martin Luther King Jr.

[64] (King Jr., n.d.)

APPENDIX

SHORT BIOGRAPHY OF MY FATHER

Olatoye, the grandson of Atoye, the great Egba warrior who migrated from Ile-Ife to settle at Igbore Abeokuta in the latter part of the 19th century, was born on the 18th of December 1924.

His father, Adegboyega, was an industrious farmer specializing in cocoa cultivation, a lucrative venture that brought him much wealth and prosperity. His mother, Sarah Kehinde, was the daughter of an Ijesha woman from the royal house of Legun in Igbore, Abeokuta.

Olatoye was born as the fifth of his mother's eight children in Igbore-Mosafejo. He spent his childhood days in the village with his parents, who had the utmost affection for him. Despite Adegboyega's wealth, however, he wasn't keen on sending any of his children to school mainly because he had not yet embraced Christianity. Christianity had a positive influence on people's attitude towards education in those days.

Olatoye's mother greatly admired the children of her Christian brothers-in-law who were attending school. She approached her brother-in-law, Omotesho, to solicit his help in convincing Adegboyega. Omotesho successfully persuaded Adegboyega to send Olatoye to school in January 1934.

By 1938, Olatoye had completed Standard III, the highest attainable grade at African Church School, Igbore-Robiyan. He proved to be a brilliant young lad, always at the top of the class throughout his primary school days. In 1939, he moved to the African Church School, Ijoko and African Church Central School, Agege, in 1940. Due to his exceptional character, leadership qualities and astounding academic abilities, he was appointed as the School's Senior Prefect in 1941 as he completed his Government Standard Six.

In March 1942, he secured a teaching job and began his glorious 40-year career as an educationist. In the first twenty months of his appointment, he taught at three different schools, including his alma mater, The African Church Central School, Agege, at the request of his former headteacher.

In 1944, the death of his sister Abiola, the mother of the late Chief B.B Majekodunmi (Founder, Ifako International Schools), plunged the family into deep sorrow. Despite the emotional trauma and strain, Olatoye emerged as the only successful candidate in the Agege LGA for the Government Teacher Training College entrance exam.

Just as he was about to graduate from college in 1946, another tragedy struck when his brother Joel Olugoyinbo died. Joel was a prominent produce merchant, an emerging star expected to redeem the clan economically. The family's financial burden fell on Olatoye's shoulders, and he did not disappoint. He successfully cleared all his late brother's trade debts and took charge of his nephews and nieces while supporting his own siblings.

Olatoye sought and got a transfer to teach at Saviors' African Church, Ikirun, where he built a solid base to launch him into the orbit of greatness. He arrived with a Teachers Grade III certificate. By 1951, he attained the Grade II Teachers Certificate, passed the London Matriculation Examination and obtained the Senior Cambridge School Certificate. As a testament to his academic ingenuity, he attempted and passed the Higher Level without taking the Lower-Level exam.

In 1952, The African Church Teachers College, Ifako, which had closed down for 12 years, re-opened. Olatoye Adegboyega, as he was then known, joined the staff. He was assigned to teach English Language, Physical & Health Education and Agriculture. Also a housemaster, he laid the strong foundation of discipline for which the college became reputed.

In 1953, Olatoye left for Fourah Bay College, Freetown, Sierra Leone, the first western-style university in West Africa. Olatoye majored in Economics, with minors in English, French, German, Law and Political/Constitutional History. His four-year course led to a Bachelor of Arts, B.A. (Hons) in Economics from the University of Durham, England. He was such an exceptional scholar.

Sadly, his beloved mother died in 1956 while he was in Freetown.

When he graduated in 1957, he won the French Government medal for outstanding performance and excellence in the French language. He was also the chief judge of the Student Representative Council. He returned to Nigeria that same year and rejoined the staff of African Church Teachers College Ifako as a French, German, Latin and English Language (and Phonics) graduate teacher. In January 1960, he was appointed as the Vice-Principal of Manuwa Memorial Grammar School, Okitipupa.

On January 8th, 1962, the Board of Governors of the African Church Teachers College recalled Olatoye from Okitipupa after Mr F.O.C Nwankwo resigned as the Principal. Olatoye assumed the position and, in his nineteen years as College Principal, built a blistering and unparalleled reputation in the history of Teacher Education. Reputed for his hard work, honesty, transparency, accountability, selflessness and integrity, his sterling performance defied explanation in the face of the prevalent moral decadence and social malaise. Through his actions and lifestyle, he readily became a legend in educational circles.

In 1969, as the Education Secretary for the African Church Organisation, he founded the Lagos African Church Grammar School (LAFROGRAMS), the school later attended by his son, Tola. His educational contributions to society gained him national and international recognition. In 1975, he embarked on an educational tour of eight American states and Canada, where he lectured at Morehead State University in Kentucky, USA. In recognition of his sterling educational leadership qualities, he was recognized and listed in the Dictionary of African Leaders and statesmen[65]. This publication included the biographies of the likes of Mandela, Julius Nyerere and other notable African leaders.

By the time Olatoye exited as the College's principal in 1981, he had carved a niche for himself and the College, which became the standard by which others were measured – a model institution. After few more years as the Executive Secretary of the Schools Management Committee and the Chief Inspector of Education, he retired from education, having become a phenomenon. In fact, he was nominated for the

In life, Olatoye was an inspiring icon. In death, he remains a living legend. His life was one of principle and integrity. The perfect gentleman who preferred to be unjustly scorned than do anything unethical or immoral, Olatoye never did anything that violated his cherished values system. This was why he earned immense admiration, acclaim, and respect from all those who interacted with him.

He was a man of distinction, who will be forever remembered by all his children – not just those from his loins, but those he nurtured to success in various fields throughout his life as a distinguished linguist, educationist par-excellence and leader extraordinaire. Olatoye passed away at the age of 86, on the 11th June 2011. He is survived by his eleven children, grandchildren and great-grandchildren. The children are:

1. **Olufunlola Soyemi:** (Retired Educationist)
2. **Aderonke Makanjuola:** (Retired Permanent Secretary, Ministry of Education, Science and technology and

[65] Published around 1974. Now out of print.

Executive Chairman of Oyo State universal basic Education)

3. **Oluranmilowo Haastrup: (**Retired Educationist, Former Secondary School Principal)
4. **Dr. Olusunmola Osinubi:** (UK- based Educational Consultant and entrepreneur)
5. **Dr. Oludamilohun Adeliyi**: (US-based Pharmacist and minister)
6. **Olufisola Adeduntan**: (Linguist and business entrepreneur based in Ireland)
7. **Olugbotola (Tola) Adeliyi**: (Teacher, Author, Speaker, and businessman, UK/Dubai)
8. **Oludamisi Alo:**(Chattered Accountant, Business entrepreneur)
9. **Oludayo Abvuere**: (US based Physiotherapist, Author and Business entrepreneur)
10. **Olufisayo Adeliyi:**(US based Metallurgical and Material Engineer, Author, Businessman)
11. **Olutomiwa Adeliyi**:(Canadian based Chattered Accountant)

And YES! We are a football team! 😊

Olatoye Adeliyi in the 60s

ABOUT THE AUTHOR

Tola Adeliyi is a science teacher, motivational speaker, and life and youth impact coach. An Animal Biology graduate from the University of Agriculture, Abeokuta, Nigeria, he was a managing partner at Archon Ventures Ltd and Golden Domains Ltd in Lagos, Nigeria. He also led a team of over 2,000 representatives at ForMor International in Conway, Arkansas.

Tola further qualified as a teacher with a Post Graduate Certificate in Education from the University of Warwick, England. During his teaching career in schools across the United Kingdom, he was a Special Educational Needs Coordinator (SENCO) and the Director of Excellence department at the Hazeley Academy, Milton Keynes, a SENCO at Thamesmead School, Shepperton, Surrey, and Assistant Head Teacher in charge of Inclusion and Special Educational Needs at Broomfield School, Enfield, London.

He is widely travelled and frequently involved in organising and giving talks on motivation and healthy living to audiences of between 50 and 1000 delegates in more than 45 countries across 4 continents. He holds regular motivational speeches to encourage young people and older groups to be purposeful and achieve their full potential.

Tola is the founder and CEO of Oxford Dream Academy, a cultural and motivational summer school, and Impact for Success, a platform for speakers, trainers, and life coaches based in England and Dubai.

"Echoes of my Father" is Tola's third published book. The first two being "*Dreams can still come true" and Medicine for the youthful mind* (A motivational Book for Teenagers and Young Adults).

Tola Adeliyi, 2021

For more information
about the book or about speaking engagements:

Visit: www.impact4success.ae or email info@impact4success.ae

www.tolaadeliyi.com or email: tola@tolaadeliyi.com or
tolaadeliyi@gmail.com

www.facebook.com/deetolaadeliyi

www.instagram.com/tolaadeliyi

Tel: +447850348800

Tel: +971551465850

Blurb

"You can be successful and not be significant, but you cannot be significant without being successful." – *Olatoye Adeliyi*

Echoes of My Father, a book for all ages, offers life-changing nuggets to help the reader undertake the vital process of self-reinvention into global citizenship. To thrive in this brave new world, you must be socially confident, articulate, and self-aware. You have to be aspirational and driven while balancing success against significance. *Echoes of my Father* offers intelligent reflections around these themes and more.

Tola Adeliyi presents a strong case for remaining positive and being proactive. He offers unique, resourceful, and time-tested strategies, based on life lessons taught by his father, to help you transition from a dreamer to a legacy-builder. It is indeed a must-read for those who seek to follow a more excellent way.

BIBLIOGRAPHY

Adams, J. Q. (n.d.). *Leadership Development 2*. Retrieved April 25, 2021, from Business Performance Improvement Resource (BPIR): https://www.bpir.com/leadership-development-2-bpir.com/menu-id-71/words-of-wisdom.html

Ali, M. (2010 , August 10). *Champions aren't made in the gyms. Champions are made from something they have deep inside them – a desire, a dream, a vision. ~Muhammad Ali.* (J. Morris, Editor) Retrieved April 24, 2021, from Wellness Words of Wisdom: https://sophia.smith.edu/blog/wordsofwisdom/2010/08/10/champions-arent-made-in-the-gyms-champions-are-made-from-something-they-have-deep-inside-them-a-desi

Ali, M. (n.d.). *Quotable quotes*. Retrieved April 24, (2021, from https://www.goodreads.com: https://www.goodreads.com/quotes/121663-impossible-is-just-a-big-word-thrown-around-by-small

Ali, M. (n.d.). *Quotable Quotes*. Retrieved April 24, 2021, from https://www.goodreads.com: https://www.goodreads.com/quotes/72164-i-hated-every-minute-of-training-but-i-said-don-t

Aristotle. (n.d.). *Aristotle > Quotes > Quotable Quote*. Retrieved April 24, 2021, from www.goodreads.com: https://www.goodreads.com/quotes/80461-excellence-is-never-an-accident-it-is-always-the-result

Boom, C. T. (n.d.). *Corrie Ten Boom Quotes.* Retrieved April 24, 2021, from www.brainyquote.com: https://www.brainyquote.com/quotes/corrie_ten_boom_135203

Bradberry, T. (n.d.). *Putting Our Problems into Perspective.* Retrieved April 24, 2021, from https://medium.com: https://medium.com/swlh/putting-things-into-perspective-b636d70a1e4c

Brown, L. (n.d.). *LES BROWN "GHOSTS" SPEECH.* Retrieved April 24, 2021, from https://motivationalwisdomblog.wordpress.com: https://motivationalwisdomblog.wordpress.com/2016/05/29/les-brown-ghosts-speech/

Cabot, M. (n.d.). *Meg Cabot > Quotes > Quotable Quote.* Retrieved April 24, 2021, from https://www.goodreads.com: https://www.goodreads.com/quotes/572007-courage-is-not-the-absence-of-fear-but-rather-the

Caine, M. (n.d.). *The First Step Toward Success – Mark Caine.* Retrieved April 24, 2021, from Due.com: https://due.com/blog/the-first-step-toward-success-mark-caine/#:~:text=%E2%80%9CThe%20first%20step%20toward%20success,which%20you%20first%20find%20

Churchill, W. (n.d.). *Success Is Not Final, Failure Is Not Fatal.* Retrieved April 24, 2021, from wanderlustworker.com: https://www.wanderlustworker.com/success-is-not-final-failure-is-not-fatal/

Coolidge, C. (n.d.). *Calvin Coolidge Quotes.* Retrieved April 24, 2021, from brainyquote.com: https://www.brainyquote.com/quotes/calvin_coolidge_414555

Cuomo, M. (n.d.). *Mario Cuomo Quotes.* Retrieved April 24 , 2021, from https://www.brainyquote.com: https://www.brainyquote.com/quotes/mario_cuomo_703697#:~:text=Mario%20Cuomo%20Quotes&text=There%20are%20only%20two%20rules%20for%20being%20successful%3A%20one%

Edison, T. (n.d.). *7 Famous Quotes You Definitely Didn't Know Were From Women.* Retrieved April 24, 2021, from forbes.com: https://www.forbes.com/sites/maseenaziegler/2014/09/01/how-we-all-got-it-wrong-women-were-behind-these-7-famously-inspirin

Edison, T. A. (n.d.). *Quotes.* Retrieved April 24, 2021, from Forbes.com: https://www.forbes.com/quotes/8999/

Einstein, A. (n.d.). *Albert Einstein Quotes.* Retrieved April 24, 2021, from Brainy Quote: https://www.brainyquote.com/quotes/albert_einstein_106192

Glasow, A. H. (n.d.). *Quotes.* Retrieved April 24, 2021 , from https://meaningin.com: https://meaningin.com/quotes/arnold-h---glasow/46732-an-idea-not-coupled-with-action-will-never-get-any

Goethe, J. W. (n.d.). *Johann Wolfgang von Goethe Quotable Quote.* Retrieved April 29, 2021, from https://www.goodreads.com/quotes/7918578-if-we-treat-people-as-they-are-we-make-them

Gretzky, W. (n.d.). *Wayne Gretzky Quotes.* Retrieved April 24, 2021, from https://www.brainyquote.com: https://www.brainyquote.com/quotes/wayne_gretzky_391237#:~:text=Wayne%20Gretzky%20Quotes&text=Procrastination%20is%20one%20of%20the%20most%20common%20an

Hill, N. (n.d.). *Procrastination Quotes.* Retrieved April 24, 2021, from http://m.wishafriend.com: http://m.wishafriend.com/quotes/amp/qid/8555/

Khing, P. Y. (n.d.). *W. Michael Scott – Thoughts of the Day.* Retrieved April 24, 2021, from https://wmichaelscott.wordpress.com: https://wmichaelscott.wordpress.com/2014/01/27/success-never-comes-to-look-for-you-while-you-wait-around-youve-got-to-get-up-and-w

King Jr., M. L. (n.d.). *Martin Luther King Jr. > Quotes > Quotable Quote.* Retrieved May 05, 2021, from Goodreads.com: https://www.goodreads.com/quotes/26963-if-you-can-t-fly-then-run-if-you-can-t-run

Levin, M. (2017, 17 30). *Why Great Leaders (Like Richard Branson) Inspire Instead of Motivate.* Retrieved 04 24, 2021, from www.inc.com: https://www.inc.com/marissa-levin/why-great-leaders-like-richard-branson-inspire-instead-of-motivate.html

Longwe, D. (n.d.). *77 Quotes to Help You Find Your Life Purpose (GUIDE).* Retrieved April 24, 2021, from https://graciousquotes.com: https://graciousquotes.com/purpose/

Mandela, N. (n.d.). *9 Inspiring Nelson Mandela Quotes on Forgiveness.* Retrieved May 05, 2021, from The Borgen Project: https://borgenproject.org/nelson-mandela-quotes-on-forgiveness/

Mandela, N. (n.d.). *Quotes.* Retrieved May 03, 2021, from BrainyQuote.com: https://www.brainyquote.com/quotes/nelson_mandela_178789

McKenna, R. (n.d.). *Sacrificial Leadership.* Retrieved April 24, 2021, from www.christianleadershipalliance.org: https://www.christianleadershipalliance.org/page/SacrificialLeader

Muccino, G. (Director). (2006). *Pursuit of Happyness* [Motion Picture]. Retrieved May 05, 2021, from https://www.goodreads.com/author/quotes/7242582.Pursuit_of_Happyness

Oxford Learners' Dictionary. (n.d.). *Oxford Learners' Dictionary.* (O. U. Press, Producer) Retrieved May 03, 2021, from https://www.oxfordlearnersdictionaries.com/definition/english/gift_1?q=gift

Qubein, N. (n.d.). *Quotes/Authors/N/Nido Qubein.* Retrieved April 24, 2021, from www.quotepub.com: https://www.quotepub.com/quote/nido-qubein-for-the-timid-change-is-frightening;-for-the-comfortable-change-is-threatening;-but-for/

Richards, C. (n.d.). *Quotes.* Retrieved April 24, 2021, from CoolNSmart .com: https://www.coolnsmart.com/quote-don-t-be-fooled-by-102990/

Rohn, J. (2017, 10 31). *Uncovering the Two Keys To Leadership Legacy.* (R. Wolfson, Editor) Retrieved April 24, 2021, from www.huffpost.com : : https://www.huffpost.com/entry/uncovering-the-two-keys-to-leadership-legacy_b_59f89e89e4b0de896d3f2b7e

Rohn, J. (n.d.). *Creating Your Character.* Retrieved May 03, 2021, from http://www.appleseeds.org: http://www.appleseeds.org/rohn_create-character.htm

Rohn, J. (n.d.). *Jim Rohn > Quotes > Quotable Quote.* Retrieved May 03, 2021, from goodreads.com: https://www.goodreads.com/quotes/580967-poor-people-have-big-tv-s-rich-people-have-big-libraries

Rohn, J. (n.d.). *Read All The Books*. Retrieved 04 24, 2021, from Apple Seeds: http://206.244.99.5/rohn_read.htm

Rohn, J. (n.d.). *The Formula for Success and Failure*. Retrieved April 24, 2021, from Success Presents Jim Rohn International: https://www.jimrohn.com/the-formula-for-success-and-failure/

Rohn, J. (n.d.). *Time Management by Rhon Jim*. Retrieved April 24, 2021, from http://www.appleseeds.org: http://www.appleseeds.org/rohn_time-mang.htm

Sartre, J. P. (n.d.). *Quotable quotes*. Retrieved April 24, 2021, from www.goodreads.com: https://www.goodreads.com/quotes/52381-we-are-our-choices

Schuller, R. H. (n.d.). *Robert H. Schuller Quotes*. Retrieved April 24, 2021, from https://www.brainyquote.com: https://www.brainyquote.com/quotes/robert_h_schuller_121372#:~:text=Schuller%20Quotes&text=Anyone%20can%20count%20the%20seeds%20in%20an%20apple%2

Sinatra, F. (n.d.). *The Best Revenge Is Massive Success – Frank Sinatra*. Retrieved April 24, 2021, from https://due.com: https://due.com/blog/the-best-revenge-is-massive-success-frank-sinatra/#:~:text=%E2%80%9CThe%20best%20revenge%20is%20massive%20success.%E

Spurgeon, C. (n.d.). *Quote*. Retrieved April 24, 2021, from www.quotes.net: https://www.quotes.net/quote/44272

Thomas, E. (n.d.). *130 Eric Thomas Quotes by Amy Finn, No. 57*. Retrieved April 24, 2021, from https://www.quoteambition.com/ : https://www.quoteambition.com/eric-thomas-quotes/

Twain, M. (n.d.). *The two most important days in your life are the day you are born and the day you find out why.* Retrieved April 24, 2021, from https://philosiblog.com/: (2021, April 24)https://philosiblog.com/2013/11/15/the-two-most-important-days-in-your-life-are-the-day

Versey, J. (n.d.). *Breaking Free Quotes.* Retrieved April 24, 2021, from Goodreads.com: https://www.goodreads.com/quotes/tag/breaking-free#:~:text=%E2%80%9CNo%20matter%20the%20strength%20of,most%20never%20leave%20their%20cages.%E2%80%9D&text=%E2

Wikipedia. (n.d.). *Procrastination.* Retrieved May 03, 2021, from Wikipedia: https://en.wikipedia.org/wiki/Procrastination

Wilde, O. (n.d.). *Oscar Wilde > Quotes > Quotable Quote.* Retrieved April 24, 2021, from www.goodreads.com: https://www.goodreads.com/quotes/12620-every-saint-has-a-past-and-every-sinner-has-a

Williams, A. L. (1988). *All You Can Do Is All You Can Do, But All You Can Do Is Enough.* Thomas Nelson Publishers.

Ziglar, Z. (n.d.). *Zig Ziglar, Quotable Quotes.* Retrieved April 24, 2021, from goodreads: www.goodreads.com https://www.goodreads.com/quotes/1177933-you-can-have-everything-in-life-you-want-if-you

Lightning Source UK Ltd.
Milton Keynes UK
UKHW051546020921
389790UK00010B/18

9 781916 894105